IN HARM'S WAY

9000958194

Help for the Wives of Military Men, Police, EMTs & Firefighters

APHRODITE MATSAKIS, PH.D.

New Harbinger Publications, Inc.

W9-BPO-121

Publisher's Note

Distributed in Canada by Raincoast Books

Copyright © 2005 by Aphrodite Matsakis
New Harbinger Publications, Inc.
5674 Shattuck Avenue
Oakland, CA 94609

Cover design by Amy Shoup; Text design by Michele Waters-Kermes; Acquired by Spencer Smith; Edited by Kayla Sussell

ISBN 1-57224-400-3 Paperback

New Harbinger Publications' Web site address: www.newharbinger.com

Library of Congress Cataloging-in-Publication Data

Matsakis, Aphrodite.
  In harm's way : help for the wives of military men, police, EMTs, and firefighters : how to cope when the one you love is in a high-risk profession / Aphrodite Matsakis.
      p. cm.
  Includes bibliographical references.
  ISBN 1-57224-400-3 (pbk.)
  1. Police spouses—Psychology. 2. Military spouses—Psychology. 3. Fire fighters' spouses—Psychology. 4. Hazardous occupations—Psychological aspects. 5. Fear. 6. Stress (Psychology) I. Title.
  HV7936.P75M38 2005
  362.2'5—dc22
                                    2005014369

07 06 05

10 9 8 7 6 5 4 3 2 1

First printing

Every society depends upon the brave men and women who are willing to lay their lives on the line for the benefit of all. Their important duties require courage, dedication, and the willingness and ability to withstand hardship and uncertainty. Their partners and family members must also be courageous, loyal, hardworking, and willing to make many sacrifices. To those men and women who risk their lives daily in the military, in the police force, and in firefighting and emergency and rescue services—and to their partners and children—whose contributions and struggles need to more fully acknowledged, this book is sincerely dedicated.

Contents

Acknowledgments

This book required the efforts of many gifted and dedicated persons. I am grateful for the creative labors of Kayla Sussell whose careful and loving editing of this book contributed greatly to its organization and clarity, and to Peter Valerio, M.A., C.P.C., and Beverly Anderson, Ph.D., for their many insights into the stresses borne by those in dangerous occupations and their family members. I would also like to thank the staff of New Harbinger Publications for their support and assistance, and Maria Morel, Jessica Chin, Rebecca Lee, Catherine Stover, and Christine Paclawskyj for their research and other contributions to this book.

I owe a special debt of gratitude to my psychotherapy clients, the men and women who work or have worked in the military, police force, emergency rescue services, and firefighting departments and other lifesaving dangerous occupations and their family members. Without their willingness to share their struggles and pain with me, this book would not have been possible. They have served as models of inspiration in their efforts to bear what, for most people, would be unbearable emotional stress.

Living Under the Sword of Damocles: Four Women Tell Their Stories

An ancient tale tells of Damocles, the servant of a wealthy king. Damocles believed that if he were a king, his life would be free of struggle and pain. One day the king asked Damocles if he'd like to trade places for a day. The overjoyed servant didn't hesitate to say yes and soon found himself sitting on a majestic throne, dressed in royal robes, with many servants ready to bring him anything he wanted. But when he looked up, he also saw a huge sword hanging over his head, ready to drop and kill him at any moment. He saw that the sword, suspended from the ceiling, was supported by a single horsehair.

"This is what it's like to be a king," the king told Damocles. "You can have all the riches of the world, but there's always a sword hanging over your head. Even when you aren't looking at it, you know it's there, and that it could end your life at any moment." He meant that a king always has many enemies. His allies can turn against him without warning. Even some of his trusted advisors and officials may secretly plot against him. A king is willing to sacrifice his life for his people, yet among his people may be those who wish to overthrow him.

Anyone who works for the military, the police force, firefighting or rescue services, or in any other dangerous line of work lives under the sword of Damocles. If you love a man whose job requires him to put his life on the line, then you, like the women who share their stories below, live under the sword of Damocles too.

Note: Because the majority of persons in dangerous fields are heterosexual men, this book is addressed to heterosexual women. However, most of the material here is relevant to men and women, regardless of their sexual orientation. Furthermore, I have written primarily from the woman's point of view. Yet there are no "good guys" and "bad guys" in this book; rather, there are two people trying their best to cope with many external pressures. In cases of abuse, however, I view the woman, or the man, who is being abused as the victim.

■ Janet's Story

"I knew that marrying a marine would mean relocations and unexpected separations. But I never expected Sam to be sent to a combat zone two years before retirement! Even if he hadn't been ordered to go, he'd have volunteered. He's that patriotic, and so am I. But I'd thought my days of missing him and agonizing about his safety were almost over. After decades of service, I felt we'd done our fair share and I was angry. Then I felt guilty for being so selfish and unpatriotic. If Sam and I aren't able to go ahead with our retirement plans, I'll resent it. But that doesn't make me a bad wife or a disloyal American. Despite my personal frustrations, I've remained committed to Sam and made all the sacrifices that go along with my commitment. I'm a good wife and patriot. When I start getting upset about things, I remind myself that I married Sam and the Marine Corps by choice, and I'm just as proud of that decision today as I was in the past."

■ Alicia's Story

"Last month my husband Ron was shot during a routine traffic stop. Maybe he'll recover or maybe he'll never walk again. It's too soon to tell. I'll never leave Ron, even if he ends up brain-dead. Yet when I think of all the hopes we had for our future, I want to scream, 'It's not fair!' But I don't scream. I don't cry either. Ron has always been strong for me. Now it's my turn to be strong for him.

"If Ron's disabled, I'll have to keep working forty hours a week. I'll probably have to take care of everything else too—the car, the yard, and everything that he used to do. I just hope that between his disability check and my salary, we can meet our bills. If I have to work overtime because we need the money, I'm afraid I'll break. But I can't break, because if I do, what will happen to Ron and the children? My family is counting on me and I can't let them down."

■ Tanya's Story

"My husband Jim decided to renew his commitment to the reserves when he learned that more troops might be needed overseas. 'Who cares about losing military benefits!' I screamed at him. 'I love our country too, but there's a war over there and I don't want to lose you!'"

"You don't understand," he said. "I love the military and deep in your heart, I know you do, too, or else you wouldn't have married me. Don't worry so much. Besides, I've heard that if more reserves are needed, our unit will be one of the last to go—for reasons I can't disclose."

"Soon after Jim reenlisted, his unit was activated for an overseas assignment. Last week he was injured, but not enough to be sent home. Yet he still tells me not to worry. But I worry. I've chewed my nails down to the bone and I'm drinking more than I should.

"What helps me most is action ... fixing up the house for Jim, sending him care packages, and writing to him. Visualizing him in my mind helps, too. I even bought a rosebush and named it after him. When I look at it, I pretend he's standing next to it, smiling at me. If Jim should die, I'm not going to tell myself, 'I'm going on without him.' Instead I'll say, 'I'm going on with him, holding him as close to my heart as I can.'"

■ Monica's Story

"My children have always known that their dad could get hurt. He's been a fireman all his life and he's had a few close calls. But ever since September 11th, it's a whole new story. Whenever there's a suicide bombing on the evening news, my daughter starts asking questions like, 'Does it hurt to die? What hurts more—being buried alive or being burned alive? If a bomb goes off, will my daddy know he's dying or will he just die? If my daddy is blown up, can we have a funeral for him? Do they have funerals when there's nothing to put in the casket?'"

"My son, on the other hand, starts running around the house yelling, 'Stop being so lazy, Mom. Go get a job—right now! Quick, call up Daddy and tell him he can hide under my bed. I hate you Mom! If Daddy dies, it'll all be your fault.'"

"Telling them their father will always be safe is a lie. So what can I say to them? What can I do for them? And how can I comfort them when sometimes I'm just as scared as they are?"

Human life is fragile. Any of us, no matter how safe we think are or how carefully we live our lives, can lose a limb or meet our death at a moment's notice. But if the man you love works a dangerous job, every few weeks he sees more death and dying than most people see in their entire lifetime. Therefore, it should come as no surprise to you or to anyone else, that even though you look fine on the outside, on the inside you're not. How could you be? With your brave man so close to death's door, inevitably your life is full of huge uncertainties—and fear. You may wake up every day wondering, "Is this the day he'll be hurt or, even worse, killed?"

On the other hand, to some degree, you may have grown numb to your fear. "Always wondering, 'Is this the last time I'll kiss him good-bye in the morning?' drove me insane," said a sailor's wife. "If I don't squelch those kind of thoughts the minute they pop into my head, then my fear takes over and cuts me off from all the good things I have in my life today."

Agonizing about your partner's safety is normal, as is denying or minimizing the danger he faces. It is impossible, however, to block out the threat of harm entirely. The truth that not only his well-being, but the course of your own life, could be permanently altered by situations out of your control casts a dark cloud of emotional and financial instability over your life. Such an ominous cloud easily brings about anxiety, depression, and other forms of emotional distress for almost anyone, especially for those who are willing to sacrifice to create the best life possible for their families.

Many wives and sweethearts of men in dangerous occupations fit this description. For over thirty years I have counseled men and women in the military, the police force, and emergency medical services (EMS), firefighters, people in other dangerous occupations, and their families. In my experience, most of the committed partners were dedicated family women who had the inner fortitude to withstand the challenges that come with loving a man in a high-risk occupation. These women were also exceptionally hard workers. For the most part, the available research supports my clinical observations (Matsakis 1996; Maynard et al. 1980). Loving a man who has a dangerous occupation isn't for the fainthearted!

However, the threats to your partner's safety are not the only sources of your stress. He may work extremely long hours. Even when off duty, he may be called back to work for an emergency at any time. If he's in the military or the reserves, he may be sent overseas or away from home at a moment's notice. His return may be postponed, perhaps even more than once. You may be proud that your partner risks his life to help others or to serve his country, yet the unpredictable nature of his schedule makes planning—whether short- or long-term—difficult, if not impossible.

There are also times when the emotionally and physically draining nature of your partner's work leaves him utterly exhausted. At times, he may come home too tired, restless, irritable, or preoccupied with his work to be as close to you as the two of you might wish. If he has learned to cope with his job stress by turning off his emotions at work, it may be hard for him to switch gears and turn them on when he's at home. You may understand rationally that his lack of energy for your relationship has more to do with the pressures of his job than his feelings for you. But emotionally, you can still feel rejected, disappointed, and lonely.

Your partner may be on emotional and physical overload, but so are you. When he works long hours or at an out-of-town assignment, you are the one who manages the home, the car, the finances, and other domestic matters. If you have children, the responsibility of attending to their many needs may fall squarely on your shoulders. You may value your partner's work, yet, at times, the loneliness can feel almost unbearable.

At first, his career seemed so exciting. You admired his courage and dedication and were so proud to be with someone committed to such important work. But now you may be wondering how long you can endure the strain of worrying about his safety.

ANXIETY AND STRESS REACTIONS ARE NORMAL

Regardless of how dedicated you are to your relationship, inevitably there will be times when you feel you just can't cope—when the lack of emotional and sexual intimacy, the fear, the workload, and the sheer loneliness, combined with the normal hassles of everyday life, simply overwhelm you. You may feel like crying, screaming, throwing things, or just staying in bed with the covers pulled over your head until you can pull yourself together.

This is how the wife of a police officer puts it: "Everyone thinks I'm a supermom, and in many ways I am. But I still get the jitters and the blues—a lot. I'm a mess for a few days, then I pull myself together and do what I have to do. It's not the work that saps my soul, although that's a part of it. It's knowing how easily my husband could be killed or hurt—by people who don't even know his name and wouldn't care about him even if they did."

Studies of military and police wives and girlfriends have found that they pride themselves on being self-reliant and supportive partners and on keeping their family together. Yet, these women also report that, at times, they feel helpless, depressed, and alone (Matsakis 1996). Many also suffer from stress-related medical conditions like headaches. There is no shame in having such reactions. Hundreds of research studies indicate such reactions are to be expected in situations of emotional or physical overload or in situations where one has little or no control over an important aspect of one's life (Van der Kolk, McFarlane, and Weiseath 1996).

HEROES AND HEROINES

In our society, stress symptoms, whether emotional like anxiety attacks or physical like shoulder pain, are increasingly seen as normal. Yet you may feel ashamed of having stress reactions anyway; with good reason. Just as your partner is expected to be a hero, you may be expected to be a heroine too. For example, he may be expected to persevere in the face of fear, fatigue, or other human limitations; and to put the mission (whether it be saving an accident victim or completing a military operation) and the needs of the group ahead of his own needs and goals. In his line of work, complaining about hardships or being concerned about personal desires may be viewed as dishonorable, if not outright disloyal.

Those same standards also may apply to you. You may be expected to fulfill your duties and support your partner, enduring all strains and sacrifices without complaint or any outward sign of distress. Living with the impossible expectation that you will be a hero or heroine all the time is a tremendous burden for both of you. Even if you don't hold yourself to such standards, others might, and they may criticize you when you fail to live up to them.

When Stress Creates More Stress: A Vicious Cycle

Ongoing stress can lead to stress reactions, which create even more stress. At the very least, having a stress reaction (such as digestive problems or migraine headaches) makes it harder for you to do your work and enjoy life. If your stress reaction requires professional care, this involves an outlay of time and money, which is stressful in and of itself. Furthermore, if you (or the people who matter to you, or those who have power over your life) view your normal stress reactions as signs of weakness, selfishness, or disloyalty, the self-condemnation that follows can lead to even more stress reactions. These, in turn, can create more self-doubts, social disapproval, and problems in functioning, which can result in even more stress symptoms, and so on. Thus a vicious cycle is established, where stress leads to more stress reactions, which in themselves create more stress and then even more stress reactions.

If you've experienced the snowballing effects of this vicious cycle or other forms of intense stress in your private moments, you may feel a troubling degree of despair and personal insecurity. You also may be looking for ways to bring more joy and peace into your life. Perhaps you decided to buy or borrow this book at that point. Yet, you may have done so reluctantly, with a sense of shame or guilt, because heroes and heroines aren't supposed to ask for help. They're supposed to solve their problems by themselves.

However, seeking help is a sign of strength, not of weakness. It shows your determination to improve your situation, and your hope that maybe, just maybe, you might find a suggestion or two that might be helpful. After all, you may have decided, "I have to have hope." And hope there is: not to protect your partner from all harm, but to increase your ability to contend with the most stressful and painful situation that anyone with the courage and inner strength to commit herself to a long-term relationship can ever encounter.

HOW THIS BOOK CAN HELP YOU

The purpose of this book is to help you appreciate your strengths and to learn how to expand upon those strengths by developing coping skills for dealing with some of the most difficult aspects of loving someone with a dangerous occupation. More specifically, this book can help you improve your ability to cope with your fears about your partner's safety, with transition times, with sexual problems, and with loneliness on holidays and other special occasions when your partner is working. It also can help you to take control over those parts of your life in which you do have some control. It can help you improve your time and money management skills, and instruct you in helping your children deal with their concerns about their father's safety. It can show you how to develop and use a support system in your community. Furthermore, in the event that your partner is disabled or killed, this book can help you develop an action plan to deal with that dreadful possibility.

This book is not a guide for recovering from trauma, depression, alcoholism, or any other addiction. If you or a family member is experiencing any of these problems, any other type of severe emotional distress, or physical or sexual abuse, the help of a qualified mental health and medical professional will be needed. Assistance in finding help for these and other related concerns not covered in this book can be found in appendix 2, Resources, at the back of the book.

HOW THIS BOOK IS ORGANIZED

All the chapters are focused on the most common problems confronting partners of persons in dangerous occupations: fear (chapters 1–4), planning for the unthinkable (chapter 5), emotional stress (chapter 6), loneliness (chapter 7), sex and sexual jealousy (chapter 8), time and money (chapter 9), children (chapter 10), and homecoming readjustment issues (chapter 11). Each chapter describes the problem area and provides suggestions and exercises to help you develop coping skills in that particular area. Appendix 1 offers guidance in effective communication, and appendix 2 provides information for finding helpful organizations, books, and professional care.

As you read, you may find that you don't share the views or concerns of some of the women whose experiences contributed to this book. This is to be expected, given that the book is based on clinical experience with and the available research on women from a wide variety of backgrounds. Feel free to skim over those parts of a chapter that don't apply to you or that conflict with your goals, values, or personality. Be careful, however, not to skim over certain sections because they touch upon difficult and painful issues that you may naturally wish to avoid. Sometimes, we often resist what we need most.

KEEPING A JOURNAL

To achieve any long-term reduction in the amount of anguish you suffer, you must complete the writing assignments. For that reason, you need to keep a separate journal that will consist of all the writing you will do to complete the exercises. Even if you already keep a personal diary, you will need to have a separate journal to work with this book for maximum benefit. I recommend buying an 8½ by 11-inch notebook because some exercises instruct you to divide a journal page into columns.

CAUTIONS

While you are working with this book, if you experience any of the following reactions, seek professional help immediately and do not continue with this text without first consulting your physician or a licensed mental health counselor: memory problems; feeling disoriented or out of touch with reality, even temporarily; suicidal or homicidal thoughts; self-destructive behavior, such as substance abuse or self-mutilation; hyperventilation or extreme nausea; hemorrhaging or uncontrollable shaking; irregular heartbeat; increased symptoms of a preexisting medical or psychiatric problem; or any intense, new, or unexplained pain.

You can expect to feel sad, anxious, numb, angry, or confused as you work with this book. At times, your emotions may even feel overwhelming. Do not become alarmed at having such strong emotions if they subside within a short time and if you regain enough emotional and mental balance so that you can function. However, if your emotions take a long time to subside or if they do not subside enough for you to resume functioning, you must contact a mental health professional immediately or go to the emergency room of a local hospital.

A FINAL NOTE

No self-help book, regardless of its quality, is a substitute for individual, couples, or family counseling. During times of extreme stress or loss, you may need the assistance of a qualified medical or mental health professional and, if you wish, a spiritual advisor as well. As you work through this book, you may find that a particular coping skill isn't helpful to you. If so, this may reflect the unique aspects of your situation, as well as the fact that there are no simple solutions for the complex problems confronting a woman in your situation. Furthermore, no amount of stress management can eliminate the dangers that face your partner. However, by increasing the number of coping techniques at your command and ridding yourself of energy-draining ways of approaching your difficulties, you can lighten some of your burdens.

CHAPTER I

What Is Fear?

Sometimes we can push our fearful thoughts out of our minds, other times they refuse to leave. Even worse, they may begin multiplying, thus creating another fear—fear of fear itself—the fear that our fears can increase to the point where they dominate our existence. The first step toward preventing our fears from controlling our lives is to listen to them. Fighting our fears only makes them stronger.

FEAR IS OUR FRIEND: THE SURVIVAL VALUE OF FEAR

Strange as it sounds, fear is our friend. If our prehistoric ancestors hadn't been afraid of large animals, we might not have survived as a species. Just as physical pain warns us of a potential medical problem, fear warns us of possible danger, thus giving us time to prepare.

Sometimes even a split second's warning can mean the difference between life and death.

Since fear is part of our innate survival system, we don't make a conscious decision to be afraid. We do so automatically in response to someone or something we perceive as a threat. The key word here is "perceive": for it's possible to be frightened by a situation we perceive as threatening, but which, in reality, poses little or no threat. However, this is not true in your case, where the threat of harm to the man you love is all too real.

Although feeling fear is designed to help protect us, sometimes the opposite is true. Fear can also propel us into a such a high state of anxiety that our thoughts become scattered; our movements erratic; and our judgement poor. Alternatively, fear can plummet us into such a state of emotional, physical, or mental numbing that it's hard to think clearly or have the energy to complete a task. Either way, run-away fears can leave us prone to having accidents and making mistakes or, the opposite, being paralyzed and unable to make necessary decisions.

But we are not helpless victims of fear. As you will see, there are many ways of managing the two most troublesome reactions to fear: anxiety and numbing. Some people find that if they allow themselves to fully experience their anxiety or numbing, without judging these feelings or doing anything to make them go away, they sometimes lift on their own (Winston 2001). However, sitting with these painful reactions until they subside may not be an option for you. If so, after completing the two exercises that follow, "Ways to Calm Yourself," and "Ways to Ground Yourself," you will have identified several ways to manage these feelings.

Furthermore, we have another survival mechanism: our minds. The next three chapters will guide you in using your mind to manage your fears. The goal of chapter 2 is to increase your awareness of your fears by putting them into words. In chapters 3 and 4, you will examine the validity of your fear and you will identify areas where you can take action to ease your fear. According to an ancient myth, the goddess Thetis tried to protect her son from harm by bathing him in the river Styx, which could transform mortals into immortals. Unlike Thetis, you have no magic powers and many of the forces that could harm your partner are beyond human control. However, there may be some ways to make him safer. No matter how few those options may be, it is important to recognize them and, if possible, to act on them.

DENIAL: FRIEND AND FOE

As you work through this book you will be asked to list your fears regarding your partner's safety. This will not be easy. Putting your fears on paper can make them seem more real. You might begin to write, then stop, terrified by the realization that you have more fears than you knew. Or you may become terrified by the recognition that you and the man you love are vulnerable to forces beyond your control. That might tempt you to assure yourself that the possibility of his being injured is so slight, it's not worth thinking about. This is a form of denial.

You also might slip into another form of denial, one based on the "just-world philosophy." This philosophy holds that people get what they deserve and deserve what they get: that is, if you are sufficiently careful, intelligent, moral, or competent, you and your loved ones can avoid harm. Thus people who are harmed (or whose loved ones are harmed) are seen as causing their misfortune by being weak, ineffectual, or somehow deserving of punishment.

If, on some level, you accept this philosophy and you also view your partner as honorable, capable, and a careful worker, you may feel confident that he will be protected. Determined not to contribute to his misfortune, you may resolve to be honorable, capable, and careful, too. These are worthy goals. However, the tragic truth is that injury and death sometimes result from random, impersonal forces that have little or nothing to do with the victim's integrity or that of his loved ones.

The just-world philosophy isn't "bad." Neither is denial. They help us to function. If we were constantly thinking about the possibility of being harmed, we might never want to leave the safety of our homes. However, unacknowledged fears tend to fester and grow. In this sense, the person who can admit to having fears is less fearful than the one who denies all fear.

In our culture, however, denial is the norm. Contemporary values tend to put happy faces on most aspects of life. In the media, death is usually portrayed as either quick or painless, and seldom as unjust. Rarely do we see a wounded soldier who dies a slow, painful, and lonely death because he is unreachable by medical care; a policeman who suffers a permanent setback after a traumatic experience; or any other form of long-term suffering. "Many of us are mortified by the tender places our fears reveal—as if our greatest terror is having it known that we are afraid at all," writes Britt (2003, p. B4). To admit to being afraid is to admit being vulnerable, which, in a culture that values strength and power, can be a source of much shame.

Our culture also values rationality and logic. Fear, however, by its very nature, isn't always logical. Hence, when you speak openly about your fears, some will call you a coward, a hysteric, overly emotional, morbid, or "too negative." Hopefully, such critical responses will not prevent you from taking the necessary steps toward managing your fears.

COPING WITH ANXIETY

When you begin working with this book, you may feel your heart begin to beat a little faster. You may also start to experience other physical signs of anxiety, like nausea; sweating; difficulties concentrating; rapid, shallow breathing; rapid or slurred speech; racing or scattered thinking; hot and cold flashes, light-headedness or dizziness; tremors or shaking; fear of losing control, going crazy, or dying; or fatigue and body aches, especially stomachaches and headaches.

Having one or more of these noticeable physical reactions is to be expected. If, however, at any time, you feel overwhelmed or develop any of the symptoms listed in the Cautions section in the introduction, stop working with this book immediately and follow the directions provided for you in the Cautions section. Even if your reactions are not very strong, you may need to calm yourself before you continue working with the exercises.

A Note of Caution: In some cases, the physical changes resulting from self-calming techniques may interact negatively with certain medical conditions or with particular medications. Before you begin any of the self-calming methods suggested here or in the resources listed in appendix 2, get the approval of a medical or mental health professional.

TIME-TESTED WAYS TO CALM YOURSELF

Writing, sharing with others, exercise, meditation, yoga, muscle relaxation, and controlled breathing have been used for calming for centuries throughout the world. Visualizing a safe place you can go to regardless of your circumstances, or visualizing someone or something you love, such as your pet or your garden, can be soothing. (See appendix 2 for books on self-calming.)

These methods can be used in an emergency. However, they are most effective when they are practiced daily so that, over time, they result in an overall decrease of bodily tension that is demonstrated by a more normal blood pressure and heart rate. This decreased level of physical tension has many excellent effects, particularly that your reactivity to fear can be reduced somewhat, permitting you to think more clearly.

Quick Fixes: These quick fixes may seem superficial when you first read them, but they might get you through moments of mounting fear and anxiety.

Place your right hand near the top of your left breast, rub your fingers gently in a circle, and say out loud at least three times, "Even though I am afraid, I completely accept and love myself"; watch five minutes of television or a video; listen to music; pick up a spoon and pretend it is holding hot tea, then blow on the spoon slowly so as not to spill the tea; complete a small chore; drink a cup of tea or warm milk; think about people, music, places, smells, foods, other aspects of your life, or any memories that give you comfort and hope; tend to a pet; do something for someone else; ask others what they do to help calm themselves.

Using these techniques only during emergencies won't permanently lower your level of body tension. Using them frantically may even increase your level of anxiety. However, if you use them with an attitude of accepting your anxiety, in a pinch they can be beneficial.

EXERCISE: Ways to Calm Yourself

In this exercise, you will create a list of possible ways you can manage anxiety. In your journal, start a new page. Call it, "Ways to Calm Myself," and make a list of any self-calming methods you've used in the past that were helpful to you. Then, select four or five of the self-calming methods described above that you think might be helpful and try them out. Disregard any suggestion that reminds you of any negative experiences or of the dangers to your loved one. You may need to experiment with a number of methods to determine which work for you. After you've tried them, add the techniques that proved helpful to you to your list.

Make copies of your list and keep it where it is handy to see. Practice and become familiar with all the techniques on your list. There is no guarantee that a method that usually helps you will always do so. On particularly stressful days, you may need to repeat a specific technique (or several techniques) until you regain some emotional balance.

COPING WITH NUMBING AND DISSOCIATION

When thinking or writing about the possibility of losing your partner, instead of becoming anxious, you may go numb. Or perhaps you become numb after a period of high anxiety. Either reaction is normal.

Numbing or dissociation, commonly referred to as "shutting down," "spacing out," "zoning out," or "going fuzzy," are forms of blocking. The blocking can be partial or total, and physical, mental, or emotional, or some combination of the three. Going numb doesn't mean you no longer care about what happens to your partner. Quite the opposite: numbing reflects not only the biological changes that occur during extreme fright, but also the wish that the danger facing your loved one didn't exist.

When Dissociation Is Severe

Everybody dissociates to one degree or another some of the time. To occasionally misplace your keys is normal. However, misplacing your keys every third time you need them is a sign of severe dissociation needing professional care. Other kinds of severe dissociation that require prompt attention include the following: frequent sleepwalking or traveling away from home without remembering your name or how you arrived at your present location; "losing time," that is, suddenly noticing that some time has passed and you can't remember what occurred; feeling no emotion for long periods of time; not experiencing physical pain or extreme heat or cold when you would normally be expected to experience them; and any form of numbing that poses a potential danger to yourself or others.

Ways to Ground Yourself

Listed below are some ways to ground yourself in reality and in the present.

Physical Grounding: Change your clothes; take a bath; touch a safe item (a chair, your clothing, hair, or shoes) or a familiar item associated with comfort (a stuffed animal, pictures of people you love); exercise; do some mindless chores; brush your teeth; apply hand or body lotion; drink water; wiggle your fingers or toes; focus your eyes on a safe item in the room; play loud music or ask whomever is with you to talk a little louder; walk around the room; brush or pet your cat or dog; play a musical instrument; or say your name out loud several times. (Keep safe and comforting items, such as stuffed animals, nearby in case you need them.)

Emotional Grounding: Talk to someone, write, pray; write yourself a letter or e-mail and send it to yourself; make contact with nature; play a musical instrument; or make a list of five people you love and say, "I love you" out loud to each person on your list.

Mental Grounding: Describe the room you are in—the colors, furniture, size, and shape (aloud or in writing); read aloud from a magazine or book; say the names of your relatives, friends, or favorite flowers or foods; sing; describe the weather; describe your plans for the rest of the day; or say out loud the date and time.

Do not: Drive (a car, truck, airplane); ride a bike or motorcycle; cook; stand on ladders; go mountain climbing, swim, ski, or engage in any sport that requires focus, balance, or concentrated effort; babysit children; handle scissors, saws, or potentially dangerous items; handle glass or other fragile items, chemicals, or weapons; make any major decisions or commitments. Avoid any people, images, places, objects, activities, or experiences that remind you in any way, however small, of a stressful event or danger to your loved one.

EXERCISE: Ways to Ground Yourself

This exercise is a continuation of the previous exercise. To complete this one, follow the same instructions as in "Ways to Calm Yourself," just substitute the word "grounding" for the phrase "self-calming." When you complete this exercise, you will have a list of ways to ground yourself to use when needed.

Affirmations

No matter how many self-calming and grounding techniques you master, there will be many times when you'll have to reach deep within yourself for inner strength. Affirmations can help build that strength. However, to be long lasting, affirmations must be built on reality, not on overly optimistic views of life or on the popular, but erroneous, idea that by overcoming your personal inadequacies, you can rid your life of anxiety, pain, and self-doubt. Affirmations do not have the power to protect you and your family from harm or to control other people or events. Their power lies in their ability to help stabilize your emotions and thoughts when you are bombarded with overwhelming demands on your emotional and physical strength.

The most effective affirmations are those that affirm your strengths, your potential to develop a particular positive quality, your inherent worth, the inherent worth of your partner, and the worth of your relationship with him. Affirmations can help you manage not only your fears about your partner's safety, but any fears you might have about your ability to cope with all that's expected of you; with loneliness and other forms of emotional pain; and with criticism.

Here are some samples of helpful affirmations:

Affirmations for Fear, Loneliness, and Emotional Pain: I accept reality. I am not responsible for events over which I have no control. I am learning to search for choices. I am learning to accept my feelings. I'm lucky to care enough about someone to be willing to wait for him, to share some of his burdens, to make this sacrifice. I'm in this relationship by choice. What I do matters. One day at a time, I'm doing what I can for myself and my partner. My partner's work is important, and my love and support matter to him. I'm not alone; I can ask for help. I'm loved; there are people who love me. I will take joy in my life when there is something to be joyful about. I can enjoy today as well as honor my fears. I'm capable of dealing with fear and pain as well as enjoying pleasure.

Affirmations for Self-Empowerment, Self-Care, and Self-Love: I'm learning to be loyal to myself. I have a reason for being here. It is safe to nurture myself. I deserve to nurture myself. I'm learning to listen compassionately to myself and to others. Asking for help strengthens me. I don't have to explain myself to everybody. As long as I don't hurt myself, others, or any living being, what anyone else thinks of me doesn't matter.

Affirmations for Coping with Work Overload: I can make a plan to organize my time. I can lighten up on myself and on others. I can do a cost-benefit analysis to see if something is worth the effort. I'm doing my best to create a balance between work and play in my life. If I try to do everything, I'll sabotage myself. It's okay to make a plan that doesn't commit me to give 100 percent of myself to everything I do. If I delay doing something, I can still do it. I can do something in small steps and still be organized and disciplined.

Now, on a new page in your journal entitled "Affirmations," write down five or six affirmations that might prove helpful to you. Use any of the sample affirmations you wish, changing them as needed, or create your own. The more you read or write them or speak them aloud, the more they will become a part of you. It may be helpful to write your affirmations on a note card that you can keep someplace handy for quick review. As time goes by, you may want to change your affirmations or add new ones to your list.

During times of crises, you may need to write your affirmations over and over again until you begin to feel some serenity and a sense of empowerment. Don't be ashamed if you need to fill ten pages with affirmations, or if you write them in large letters, or use colored markers. Your efforts show your determination to make yourself stronger. That holds true for any of the suggestions in this book. Practicing some of the coping skills several times before you experience any benefits is very like basic training. Just as your partner had to practice certain skills over and over during his basic training, so too you might need to practice affirming your strengths.

CHAPTER 2

The Reality of Danger: Identifying Fears

■ Denise's Story

"Waiting. All I do is wait. Monday, Tuesday, Wednesday ... a three-day eternity from hell. Is he alive or dead, in one piece, or twelve? My husband Joe is a medic. On Sunday he was flown to the countryside after some skirmishes there. No one's heard from him since. Joe's mother says, 'I'm not worried. So why are you? Now you got the kids all worked up. Denise, I've been a military wife for years. Think positive or you'll have a nervous breakdown. We haven't heard from Joe because of a communications problem. He'll be back. I know it.'

"After listening to Joe's mom I was ashamed. I was letting everyone down by worrying so much. No news is good news. Or is it? I don't know and I don't know how to know. What I do know is that all I want to do is sit by the phone and wait for news of Joe. Crazy as it sounds, I think if I sit close enough to the phone, Joe will hear me saying 'I love you.'

"'I'm not dead yet,' Joe said, after I whispered those words to him while he got ready to leave. 'And, sweetheart, if anything happens to me, don't get emotional. Be strong. But nothing's going to happen. So stop acting like you'll never see me again. It's bad luck.'

"I still don't know what's best: to think the worst and talk about it; or try to forget about it and deal with it if and when it happens. That's my life, full of questions with no answers."

What do you think? Are you more like Joe's mother, who assumes the best, or do you usually assume the worst? Perhaps, like Denise, you don't know what to think. People with dangerous jobs are killed or seriously injured every day. Yet some emerge from the deadliest dangers without a scratch. In truth, it's difficult, if not impossible, to estimate the probability that your partner will be harmed. Accident and death statistics offer some guidelines, but the situations your partner confronts are full of uncertainties.

He can be injured or killed as the result of physical assault, exposure to illness, or an accident caused by psychological stress. Psychological stress can lead to depression and emotional suffering, or to any number of stress-related medical problems. This chapter presents some of the available information on the potential threats to your partner's physical and emotional well-being and their possible impact on your well-being, as well.

THE REALITY OF DANGER

Combining all occupational groups, recent estimates indicate that approximately 5 workers per 100,000 are killed on the job every year. The overall casualty rates for those in the military are at least ten times higher; and for police, emergency medical services workers, and firefighters, two to three times higher (Maguire et al. 2002). **Military Note:** Unless otherwise noted, the Department of Defense (DOD) statistics used in this book are based on all active duty personnel, including those serving in nonhostile areas.

The Military: Between 1980 and 1999, the average casualty rate for all four branches of the military, including both hostile deaths (those caused by enemy attack) and nonhostile deaths (those caused by accident, illness, homicide, and suicide) ranged from 54.9 per year to 116.6 per year per 100,000 active duty personnel (DOD 2003a). (These figures exclude full-time guard and reserve personnel.)

During the same period (1980 to 1999), nonhostile deaths per 100,000 active duty personnel fluctuated between 9.1 and 22 per year for illness; 2 and 7.9 for homicide; and 7.9 and 15.9 for self-inflicted harm (DOD 2003b). The accident and casualty rates for specific branches of the military and for specific wars, armed conflicts, and time periods are available on the Department of Defense web page http://web1.whs.osd.mil/mmiodcasualtyucatas.

Police: The estimated fatality rate for police is 14.2 per year for every 100,000 police workers, including administrative and support staff (Maguire et al. 2002). The casualty rate for police on the streets is probably much higher. In addition, between 1990 to 2000 the assault rate for police was more than 400 percent higher than their casualty rate (U.S. Census Bureau 2002). There is little definitive data on police suicide, but it is known to be higher than the national average (Kates 2001).

Firefighters: The estimated fatality rate for firefighters is 16.5 deaths per 100,000 (Maguire et al. 2002). About 44 percent of firefighter deaths are from heart attacks; 27 percent from traumatic injuries, including internal and head injuries; and 20 percent from burns and asphyxiation (U.S. Fire Administration 2003). With the exception of those lost during the terrorist attack of 9/11, between 1992 to 2002, the percentage of paid firefighters who were injured (approximately 41 percent per year) or who were killed (about 100 per year) has remained almost the same (*The Economist* 1995). However, firefighters did battle over 30 percent more fires during this time period, which implies that they are at greater risk today than they were over a decade ago (Savoye 2002). Because many states do not track suicides by occupation, there is little data on suicide among firefighters.

Emergency Medical Services: According to statistics collected in the 1990s, being an EMS worker is almost as dangerous as being a policeman or firefighter. The fatality rate for EMS personnel is approximately 12.7 per 100,000 workers, more than double the national average of 5 for occupational deaths during the same time period (Maguire et al. 2002). EMS workers are killed by falls, electrocution, ambulance crashes, and other accidents. Like firefighters, they are subject to sudden death and other stress-related medical problems (Maguire et al. 2002). To date, there is little information on suicide rates among EMS workers. Several EMS workers who served heroically during the Oklahoma City bombing (1996), the attack on the World Trade Center (September 11, 2001), and other national disasters have committed suicide. Their individual histories indicate that they all suffered from years of chronic pain as the result of job-related injuries, or from survivor guilt or post-traumatic stress (Hopkins and Jones 2003).

No Safe Time or Place

Soldiers and police are in danger around the clock, whether on duty or not; criminals don't work from nine to five; neither do enemy soldiers. In this era of brazen, coldhearted violence and suicide bombers, horrific acts of violence take place not only at night in secluded places, but during the day in the middle of busy streets. This increases the risk of harm to soldiers, police, firefighters, and rescue workers. In addition, workers in all these fields, especially the police, are increasingly subject to attacks by the mentally ill (Lamb, Weinberger, and DeCuir 2002). Due to shrinking mental health funds, many disturbed individuals are left untreated. When they create disturbances, it's the police, EMS workers, and even firefighters who provide help.

Exposure to Illness

Workers in high-risk fields are exposed to contagious diseases and viruses, like AIDS, and to extreme temperatures and other harsh environmental conditions. Today, as in the past, soldiers sent abroad can develop lifelong health problems after being exposed to dangerous herbicides and pesticides, poison gases, malaria, tuberculosis, and parasites.

Overconfidence

Feelings of terror and powerlessness are normal reactions to witnessing or being subject to hideous injuries and death. For men with high-risk jobs, however, such feelings may be personally unacceptable. Not only do these emotions undercut the self-image of the self-confident invulnerable hero, they can also result in being shamed by peers or deemed unfit for duty. As a result, some (but not all) men put on a mask of fearlessness.

Some men develop a sense of personal infallibility and become overconfident. If your partner is overconfident, this may reduce his anxieties about the threat of harm, but not yours. If you see him neglecting certain precautions or taking unnecessary risks, your fears may rise, and justifiably so. Such overconfidence has proved to contribute to accident and casualty rates (Laws 2002).

Neglecting certain well-established cautions or taking risks that serve no purpose other than to appear brave are obviously acts of overconfidence. However, deciding whether a particular act is foolhardy or heroic is a judgment call. An EMS worker explains: "What's right and wrong when you have a split second to decide who will live or die might be totally different than what's right or wrong to someone sitting behind a desk." (See "Exercise: Encouraging Your Partner to Seek Help," in chapter 6, for suggestions for dealing with the issue of overconfidence.)

Psychological Stress

Psychological stress is a major contributor to accident and casualty rates. The emotional strains your partner encounters are many: threats to his personal safety, exposure to human injury and death (especially incidents involving children, multiple deaths, human error, or malice); instances where honest mistakes are interpreted as incompetence or willful dereliction of duty; and instances where he or others in his field are blamed for problems caused by malfunctioning equipment, incompetent leadership, inadequate training, and insufficient staff.

Especially stressful are allegations of corruption or incompetence within his working group or profession. Even when your partner is not directly involved, he may be shamed by people who generalize from the behavior a few members of a group to all of its members. Even when the allegations are dismissed as untrue, he may be unjustly condemned by those who don't understand that men in his field often confront situations where all of the available options involve violating some moral principle or standard procedure.

The resulting feelings of being betrayed, misunderstood, and unappreciated, combined with his intimate knowledge of human suffering and death, can profoundly affect his view of life. If he entered his job with a pessimistic view of life, then his work experiences may have only confirmed his negativity. If he began his career with an optimistic or semi-optimistic view of life, his work experiences may have tarnished, if not eroded, his faith in the goodness of life.

He may have lost his innocence all at once, in one shattering moment of personal horror. Or he may have lost it piece by piece, a little bit at a time.

Along the way, you may have learned more than you ever wanted to know about the fragility of life or the dark side of human nature. Even if your partner has tried to protect you by not talking about his work, you probably have a sense of what he must deal with in his work life from the media or from other sources. For some of you, this knowledge may have severely challenge certain long-cherished beliefs, such as that people are basically good. As a result, you too may have lost some, or a great deal, of your innocence.

Not every woman becomes so disillusioned. If you have, however, you may now be concerned not only about your partner's safety, but about your own, and that of your children and others you love. Furthermore, if your partner has been particularly graphic in his sharing, you may have experienced vicarious traumatization: that is, you may have been traumatized by a traumatic incident just by hearing about it.

You cannot develop a full-blown case of post-traumatic stress disorder simply by learning about another's trauma. Yet vicarious traumatization can result in you having nightmares or intrusive thoughts about your partner's traumas. You may become easily startled, or constantly be on the lookout for danger, or become obsessed with the work-related issues that trouble your partner. Unless you have a history of trauma, however, these reactions are usually short-term.

On the other hand, you or your partner may have retained your optimistic views of life, or changed them only to a limited extent. Or perhaps it is you, rather than he, who became disillusioned, and you now view his more positive outlook as naive or unrealistic. If your worldview is vastly different from your partner's, conflicts can result. Unfortunately, such disagreements become yet another source of psychological stress for both of you.

When all of these factors are combined, the many emotional injuries and pressures described here can exhaust even the toughest, most dedicated soul, as well as his partner. Your partner may have found constructive ways to offset his job stress, for example, through religious practices, sports, community activities, exercise, or other self-improvement efforts. However, some men cope by drinking, detaching from their feelings, overworking, engaging in dangerous hobbies, or displacing their frustrations onto their partner or other family members. Some indulge in sexual excesses; others lose their sexual desire (Maynard et al. 1980; Melzer 2002). Some may develop addictions, depression, or post-traumatic stress disorder (Kates 2001).

If your partner has developed any of the problems mentioned above, you may be suffering the pain of watching someone you love becoming so unhappy and exhausted. Your pain will be even greater if any of his habits are eroding his health. As one woman stated, "I'm afraid he'll break, and if he breaks, I'm afraid that I'll break watching him break." (The exercise "Encouraging Your Partner to Seek Help," in chapter 6, offers suggestions on how to encourage your partner to seek help for coping with his job-related stress.)

Note: Regardless of the stresses inherent to your partner's job, physical, emotional, or sexual abuse cannot be tolerated. If anyone in your family is troubled by any of these problems, seek legal and medical help immediately. See appendix 2, Resources, for assistance.

EXERCISE: Identifying Fears

One way to begin to deal with your fears is to list them on paper. There is power in "naming the demon." Naming it won't make it disappear, but it can give you some sense of control. At the very least, putting your fears into words can be a starting point to clearer thinking and the beginning of exploring the possible options.

Writing out your fears isn't magic: it doesn't make a particular fear less likely to come true; nor does it mean you'll never be tortured by that fear again. However, taking a particular fear out of the privacy of your darkest imaginings and writing it on paper externalizes and even objectifies your fear. If you write it down, that means you no longer have to carry the full weight of that fear solely within yourself. You can expose it to the light of day.

Part I. Identifying Your Fears: Close your eyes and think about the various fears you have about your loved one's safety. Then open your eyes and on a new page in your journal entitled "My Fears About _____'s (insert the name of your loved one) Safety," write down the first ten or twelve fears that pop into your mind. (If you don't have that many fears, don't be concerned. Just list the ones you do have.) Items on your list can be just a few words or phrases, or a sentence or two. It's important to be as concrete as is possible. For example, if you fear that "something bad will happen," try to specify what that bad event might be, such as falling into a coma due to an assault, loss of a limb or even two, brain damage, blindness, and so forth.

Part II. Selecting Your Main Fears: After writing your list, take a few deep breaths and review it. Which five of these fears cause you the most concern? (If there are fewer than five fears on your list, simply consider those your main fears.) To select the fears that are most important to you, let your emotions guide you, not your mind. Don't exclude a strong fear because someone else thinks it's stupid or irrational. Often, so-called "irrational" fears cause much suffering, and, in this world of surprises, they might not be as irrational as you may think.

For example, Denise listed the following fears for her husband as causing her the most distress: (1) being shot by enemy soldiers; (2)

drowning; (3) being in a helicopter or car crash; (4) becoming a prisoner of war; (5) being burned alive in an explosion. Also, Denise had often worried about Joe being bitten by a poisonous snake and that he'd be too busy tending to others to take care of himself. Compared to her other fears, this seemed silly to her, and even sillier to her friends. But, when she dismissed this fear, she failed to recognize that she knew him best. Therefore she, not others, was most likely to best predict how Joe might react under pressure.

As it turned out, during a battle, Joe was indeed bitten by a poisonous snake and, if not for the insistence of a team member, he would have delayed treating the bite to tend to the needs of the badly wounded. Joe had to be evacuated by helicopter and rushed to a hospital for care there.

Like Denise, you are the expert on your partner's behavior. In examining your fears, respect your intimate knowledge of his personality, strengths, and weaknesses. Others may have valuable insights, but don't forget to listen to yourself. Even if others have positive proof that one of your fears is ridiculous, if that fear still causes you great distress, you need to pay attention to it.

Part III. Clarifying Your Main Fears: Now, rewrite the fears you identified in Part II in the form of one or two complete sentences. This will help you be more specific about your fears. If you've already listed your major fears in sentence form, disregard these instructions and move on to the next chapter.

CHAPTER 3

Examining Your Fears

Sometimes our fears come to us as fleeting thoughts; other times, as a sequence of events, similar to a scenes from a movie where the heroine's life hangs by a thread. This horror movie may be a stream of consecutive events or it may appear in bits and pieces. Have such terrible visions ever invaded your mind? Were there times you couldn't rid yourself of these horrible visions no matter how hard you tried? Do you now fear having more "fear attacks" and wonder how you will be able to function if they become more frequent or long lasting?

Some of the self-calming and grounding techniques described in chapter 1 can help you manage these "fear attacks." In this chapter you will learn one more (three-part) method for controlling your fears: you will (1) write down your fears in detail; (2) break down each fear into separate smaller pieces (subfears); and (3) examine each separate subfear for its meaning and validity.

THE VALUE OF BREAKING DOWN BIG FEARS INTO SUBFEARS

Tackling all your fears at once can be overwhelming. It is much easier to manage them by breaking them into smaller units or subfears. As you closely examine each subfear (one at a time), you may be able to dismiss some of them as highly improbable. Also, you may discover ways to help avert the disaster you anticipate. Completing this process cannot eliminate your fears about your partner's safety, for his job is dangerous. However, it will prevent your fears from spiraling into an unmanageable whirlwind of terror and your burden of fear will feel lighter.

EXERCISE: Breaking Down Fear into Separate Pieces

Set aside a new page in your journal entitled "Breaking Down Fear into Separate Pieces" and follow the directions below:

1. Review the list of five major fears that you identified in the last exercise in chapter 2.

2. Select one of these on which to focus. (Later, if you choose to, you can complete this exercise with one or more of the other fears that appear on your list.)

3. Underneath the heading, copy your description of the fear you've selected. For example, " I am afraid _____."

4. Next, close your eyes and take a few deep breaths. Then open your eyes and ask yourself, how many different ways have you imagined this particular fear becoming a reality? For instance, if

you decided to focus on your fear of your partner drowning, ask yourself in what specific ways might this nightmare occur? Will he drown trying to save a life or will he be purposely drowned by an assailant? Will he be alone or with comrades? If you focus on your fear of him being shot, do you then imagine him being shot awake or asleep, at close range, or from afar?

Several different scenarios may come to mind. You can jot down some brief notes for as many scenarios as you wish; however, to complete this exercise only one scenario is necessary.

5. Review the various scenarios you've just described. Select one and break it into as many subfears as possible. If your fears contain specific locations, persons, or other particular details, include those too. Do not exclude any fears that deeply trouble you, even if you or others think they are "illogical." Sometimes these allegedly "irrational" fears are the source of great pain.

    Use as many pages as you need. You may want to write for ten minutes, and then take a break. I don't recommend writing for more than half an hour at a time.

6. After describing your fear-provoking scenarios in detail, put your journal away for a day or two. Then reread what you've written. Add any additional details or fears that come to mind.

Reviewing and rewriting your fears repeatedly may seem unnecessary. However, if you wish to manage them, you need to know what they are. The more you think and write about them, the more likely you are to access any fears that might exist below the surface. For example, Denise chose to explore her fear that her husband Joe would be captured and made a prisoner of war. The first time she broke down this fear into separate pieces, she identified several subfears, such as Joe would be badly beaten or die of malaria. After setting aside her description for a few days, Denise reviewed it. Doing that helped her to recall certain fears that she had pushed away because she saw them as too grim. Yet they had not disappeared.

EXERCISE: Recording Your Fear-Producing Events

In this exercise you will record your fear-producing scenario. First, divide your journal page into seven columns. Make columns 1, 5, and 7 narrower than the others. That's because 1, 5, and 7 need to be only wide enough to write one- or two-digit numbers or a Roman numeral. Label the column heads as follows: 1. My Feared Scenario; 2. Estimated Probability; 3. Additional Emotional Meaning; 4. Self-Blaming Beliefs; 5. Catastrophic Thinking; 6. Additional Information; and 7. Revised Estimated Probability. Because the column heads contain two or three words, stack them one on top of the other so that they will appear only on top of the intended column.

As you break down your description of the fearful scenario into as many separate pieces as possible, some of your entries will take the form of a scenario or a chronological account of what you fear might happen; others will describe fears that don't have a particular timeline or sequence. Each entry will describe a separate fear. Number each entry so you can refer to your entries in future exercises. It will look like this:

Column Numbers   1   2   3   4   5   6   7

1. **Entry Number One** I'm afraid that _____

2. **Entry Number One** I'm afraid that _____

Leave some space before and after each entry, because as you complete this exercise, you will probably remember another fear that should be included. If you like, you can approach this by imagining that you are writing a letter to a friend or a story for a newspaper about what you fear might happen to your partner. You want to follow him through each step of his ordeal. Don't be concerned if your story lacks some pieces; you can still benefit from this exercise.

When Denise began working with this exercise, she wondered if not hearing from Joe for several days meant he had been killed. But she decided to hope he was still alive and had been captured and made a prisoner of war. This is how Denise completed this exercise:

1. On the way to the prison camp, Joe is struck by so many rocks thrown by angry locals that the guards are unable to protect him. Even if they try to protect him, they fail.

2. A rock hits Joe in his eyes and his vision is permanently damaged, or he is blinded.

3. The mob grabs Joe and drowns him; or the guards drown him.

4. The vehicle carrying Joe to the prison camp is blown up by a roadside car bomb.

5. If he survives the car bomb, he'll die from his wounds, due to lack of medical attention.

6. Joe will die a slow painful death without anyone to care for him.

7. Even if there's no car bomb, once Joe arrives at the camp, he will be beaten.

8. The injuries caused by the beatings will kill him or disable him for life.

9. I'm also scared that Joe won't have access to antimalaria pills and he'll die of malaria.

10. Even if he survives the malaria, he'll have lifelong side effects from it, like brain damage.

11. Even if he has access to antimalaria pills, there aren't enough to go around. Joe is so kindhearted he'll give his pills to another POW.

12. He'll fall ill or die from the unsanitary conditions and contaminated water at the camp.

13. I won't have the money to go wherever I'll have to go to fight for Joe's freedom.

14.   Even if I can get the money, I won't be able to go, because if I do, I'll lose my job.

15.   If I can't fight for Joe, he'll be in the POW camp longer, increasing the odds he'll die.

16.   Even if he comes home alive, he'll be physically disabled and get very depressed.

A MULTITUDE OF FEARS

While Denise was writing her scenario, she discovered that she had a multitude of subfears. For example, she feared that because of Joe's depression, her children's grades would drop; that Joe wouldn't be able to love her anymore; and, as a result, she would become so distraught that she would start failing at work, then lose her job, and, finally, be unable to meet her bills. If she lost her job, she worried that she and her children would become homeless.

Discovering that she had so many fears frightened Denise. But it also gave her a sense of relief. She finally understood why her anxiety about Joe's safety sometimes immobilized her. "No wonder I'm so weepy and shaky! I have more than a dozen fears for just one of the five ways I'm most scared Joe will get hurt," Denise told a friend. "With more than sixty specific fears hitting me at the same time, I think I'm doing quite well—actually amazingly well."

Estimating Probabilities

After recording your feared events, you will be ready to estimate the probability of each separate subfear becoming a reality. On a scale of 0 to 100, with 0 percent signifying no chance of this event ever occurring, and 100 percent indicating that the event will certainly take place, estimate the probability of occurrence for each separate item and write your numerical estimate in column 2, "Estimated Probability." Remember that given the many uncertainties of your partner's work, your estimates (or those of others) cannot predict the actual probability that certain events will occur.

Additional Emotional Meaning

In this section you will explore the possibility that some of your fears may have an additional emotional impact because they are associated with situations unrelated to your fears about your partner's occupation. This doesn't mean your fears aren't "real." It means that in addition to the anxiety you are suffering because of the very real possibility that one of your worst nightmares may come true, you might be feeling more pain due to an experience unrelated to your partner's safety. Identifying all the sources of your fear can help you better understand, and accept, your emotional reactions.

This is how Denise explained it: "Sometimes I'd get more upset about Joe drowning than about him being beaten. I felt stupid for feeling this way because I knew it was much more likely that Joe would be beaten. When I reviewed item 3 on my list, however, I remembered that when I was ten, one of my classmates drowned. Now that I see my terror about Joe drowning is partly related to that incident, I feel a little less crazy." Recognizing that her fear of Joe drowning had added meanings didn't eliminate Denise's fear that Joe might drown. But she understood better why she reacted so strongly to that specific fear, and her faith in her own judgment improved.

When she reviewed items 13, 14, and 15, Denise remembered that many years ago she hadn't been able to afford to travel to attend a friend's wedding. Her friend died shortly after the wedding. As a result, Denise came to associate death with a lack of travel funds, which added to her fear that her current lack of travel funds would lead to Joe's death. After completing this exercise, Denise still believed that her lack of funds could endanger Joe's life. Yet she also understood that lack of travel funds did not automatically mean that Joe would die.

EXERCISE: Checking for
Additional Emotional Meanings

Now, return to your detailed account of your fear-provoking scenario. Examine one entry at a time and ask yourself, "Are there any aspects of this situation that remind me of a person, place, or situation that caused or is causing a strong emotional reaction?" In column 3, "Additional Emotional Meaning," write one or two sentences about any other meanings you may have regarding your fear. Remember, having added emotional meaning attached to some of your fears is neither "bad" nor "wrong." All adults associate certain emotions with their experiences.

Self-Blaming Beliefs

In our desperate need to explain how something terrible could happen to someone we love, we sometimes blame ourselves for their misfortune. For example, if we ever had a hostile wish toward that person, we might believe that our wish caused their suffering. But, unless we purposely attack that person (or conspire to do so), our wishes haven't the power to bring harm to anyone. If they did have such power, then they also could protect that person from all harm.

Another common self-blaming belief holds that the death or injury of a loved one is punishment for one's own misdeeds. This notion has no scientific merit; yet it persists. When Denise was a child, a teacher told her, "When little girls lie, something terrible happens—like their mother or father dies." As an adult, she rejected this idea. Yet when Joe was reported missing, her parents' foolish words came to her mind. She believed irrationally that if Joe were harmed, it would be retribution for the time she cheated on a high school exam.

Because Denise felt so guilty, she began to doubt her judgment. She had many ideas about how to improve her life or better manage her fears, yet she lacked the confidence to put her ideas into action. Like her, you may have some irrational self-blaming beliefs that hinder your ability to cope effectively with your fears. These beliefs can generate new fears and send your fear level skyrocketing. For example, soon after Denise began blaming herself for Joe's possible misfortunes, she became convinced that if her children were ever harmed, that would be yet another punishment inflicted on her for her past misdeeds.

EXERCISE: Checking for Self-Blaming Beliefs

Review each item on your list of fears and examine it for irrational self-blaming beliefs. If you find there is an unfounded self-blaming belief associated with a particular fear, note it in column 4, "Self-Blaming Beliefs." Write a sentence or two about it if you wish.

When Denise completed this exercise, she found a self-blaming belief in item 11, her fear that Joe would give away his antimalaria medication. "I often complimented Joe for his generosity. Maybe if I had told him to think of himself first and forget the others, he would keep the malaria pills for himself." Yet Denise cannot control Joe's behavior. Moreover, he might not be as selfless as she thinks he'd be in this situation. Or, his selflessness might lead him to keep the medication for himself. As a medic, he might think it his duty to stay alive to help others.

Catastrophizing

Overly optimistic thinking is characterized by statements like "Everything will be alright." Such thinking wrongly assumes that nothing could go wrong. In contrast, *catastrophic thinking* assumes that nothing can go right: that one negative event inevitably sets off a cascade of more negative events, ending in a situation where your partner is harmed. Catastrophic thinking is erroneous because it arrives at negative conclusions without sufficient evidence, and it disregards the possibility that taking action may avert a tragic ending.

Unhappily, however, in situations such as those that confront your family, catastrophic thinking sometimes can predict injury and death accurately. Yet some action can be taken and the horrible endings that are feared may be only several of many possible outcomes. For example, although encouraging your partner to take care of his health cannot ensure his safety, it can increase his chances of survival during surgery and other medical procedures.

EXERCISE: Checking for Catastrophic Thinking

Review your journal entries and check for evidence of catastrophic thinking. On a separate page in your journal entitled "Catastrophic Thinking," describe any catastrophic chain of events you uncovered. Include the numbers of the entries that are involved in that particular chain of events so that you can refer to them later. Number each chain of events with Roman numerals: I, II, and so forth. Then return to your record of feared events and put the Roman numeral of the appropriate description next to each entry mentioned in that description in column 5, "Catastrophic Thinking." Later on you can use this numeral to refer to the chain of catastrophic events in which it is included.

Here's an example from Denise's journal:

I.   Joe will be captured, struck by rocks, and the guards can't or won't protect him. Joe's vision will be so damaged he won't be able to work. He'll get depressed, but won't go for help, so then he'll get more depressed or start drinking.

Denise then placed the Roman numeral I in column 5 of her chart for each entry involved in the catastrophic chain of events she described in entries 1, 2, 15, and 16. Denise's vision of doom could happen; however, it is not inevitable. Every step of the way there are other possibilities, both positive and negative. One negative possibility is that Joe could be executed and never make it to a POW camp. On a more positive note, his captors might need medical professionals. Because Joe is a medic, they might do everything to protect him and keep him safe and healthy in the camp so they can make use of his skills.

Denise also assumes that without travel money, she can't help Joe; that if she asks for a leave from her job, she will lose it; that if she loses her job, her family will become very poor; that if her family is impoverished, she and her children will become homeless. Once again, there is some validity to her thinking. The chain of events she envisions has happened to others. But Denise has not considered other ways this chain of events could unfold or any action she could take to interrupt or change it.

For instance, it's possible that friends, relatives, and various military or other organizations would raise the needed funds; that someone else might be able to do the necessary traveling; that Joe can be helped in ways that do not involve travel; that her employer might grant her all the leave she needs; that even if she's fired from her current job, other employers might be proud to hire the wife of a POW; that even if she can't afford to pay the rent, her children might qualify for military benefits or other forms of financial aid.

Gathering Additional Information

The more you understand the various aspects of your fears, the greater your ability to assess the degree of danger involved and to think of ways to prevent your fear from becoming a reality. You can learn more about your partner's occupation from various sources: books, the Internet, your partner, his coworkers; publications issued by his employer (if permissible); even novels and other literature relevant to your fears. Your local librarian can offer assistance. You might want to learn more about the geographical area in which your partner works. For example, Denise was elated to discover that Joe's base camp was hundreds of miles from the nearest river, lake, or ocean. While it was possible Joe's captors might drive that far to drown him, it was highly unlikely they would go to such lengths.

After you have completed your research, briefly note new, relevant information to your record in column 6 "Additional Information."

If you find contradictory information or no information about a particular area, note this as well.

EXERCISE: Revising Probabilities

Congratulations. You've just completed a lot of work. Now you will use the results of all your hard effort to reassess your fears. Considering one entry at a time, review your notations regarding any added emotional meaning, catastrophic thinking, self-blaming belief, and new information. Based on all these factors, what is your new estimate of the probability that this fear will materialize? Place this probability estimate in column 7: "Revised Estimated Probability." Now compare this with the original estimate you made for this entry in column 2. Has your original estimate increased, decreased, or remained the same?

If your original probability estimate has decreased, you may feel relieved and overjoyed. Having found that one or more of your self-blaming beliefs, or your lack of accurate information, or your prior experiences caused you to inflate your estimate of the probability of your partner being harmed, you now may be eager to examine more of your fears using the exercises in this chapter. Should you choose to do so, realize that just because one examination of a fear yielded happy results, this doesn't mean that examining all of your fears will reduce your estimate of the probability that your man will be injured.

On the other hand, if your original estimate has increased, you now may feel more fear and despair than before you began these exercises. If you realized that your man is at greater risk than you had thought, it would be perfectly normal for this realization to send you into a state of panic or numbing. If that is the case, use the coping suggestions for anxiety and numbing in chapters 1 and 4 to help youf regain your composure.

Even if your original estimate has remained the same, you may feel a deep disappointment and you may experience increased anxiety about your partner's safety. On a deeper level, after reading this chapter, you may realize more acutely that your fear is not a fantasy, but grounded in reality. If you feel emotionally shaken, use the coping suggestions in chapters 1 and 4 to help you stabilize your emotions.

Once you have regained some emotional control, you may then be able to view your analysis of your fear as a valuable source of information. The additional insights you'll have gained as a result of examining your fear can be used to reassess your priorities and suggest possible courses of action to help your partner and your family. Furthermore, should others challenge the rationality of your fear without offering you new information, you can stand firm in your assessment of the situation and your decisions on how to best take care of yourself, your partner, and your family.

Whether your original estimate has increased, decreased, or remained the same, don't assume that examining all your fears will lead to the same outcome. If the fear you examined here is more likely than you had thought, that doesn't mean that all your fears are more likely than you had thought. Similarly, don't assume that if your estimated probability decreased, that you are probably exaggerating all of your fears. Each fear needs to be examined separately. Remember, too, that your probability estimate is based on the information you have at this particular moment. Yet anything can change at any time. The future may bring major changes in your lives, in your family and neighborhood, or in society and the world at large that could significantly influence your probability estimate.

Moreover, days or weeks after completing these exercises, you may become aware of further details about your partner's situation that you had overlooked or that were not available to you when you first did the exercise. You may become aware of added emotional meanings, irrational self-blaming beliefs, or instances of catastrophic thinking that could significantly influence your probability estimate. Such new insights are normal. If they occur, return to the exercises here and use your new insights to examine your fears once more. Unhappily, reworking the exercises in this chapter with additional information and insights may increase your probability estimate. Yet it is also possible that your assessment may remain unchanged or that, hopefully, it may decrease.

CHAPTER 4

Coping with Fear

Fear rules the lives of many people, yet often they are unaware of how their fears direct their behavior. Perhaps they're afraid to face their fears; or maybe they haven't got the tools with which to do so. You, however, have had both the courage to face your fears and the willingness to do all the hard work involved in doing the exercises in the first three chapters. You've not only identified your worst fears, you've also gathered information about them and thought about how their intensity may have been influenced by earlier life experiences or by irrational beliefs. At times, this lengthy process probably confused you. Yet you persisted. Congratulate yourself.

In this chapter you'll learn more ways to manage your fears. You will begin with one fear, the same one you analyzed in chapter 3. The same process can be applied to other fears at other times. First, you'll examine this fear to uncover any ways you can prevent it from becoming a reality. You'll also identify those aspects of this fear over which you have little or no control. Then, you'll develop action plans for the former and coping skills for the latter.

IDENTIFYING OPTIONS

Identifying your options involves applying the well-known Serenity Prayer to your fears. It goes like this: "God, grant me the serenity to accept the things I cannot change, the courage to change the things I can, and the wisdom to know the difference."

EXERCISE: Identifying Options

Now, start a new page in your journal entitled "Identifying Options" and follow the directions below:

Step 1. Turn to your journal entry for the exercise "Breaking Down Fear into Separate Pieces" in chapter 3, in which you described the fear you decided to focus on in step 3. Copy your description of this fear underneath the heading of your new journal page. For example, "I am afraid _____."

Step 2. In one or two phrases or sentences, write down three of the subfears contained within your larger fear: A. _____
B. _____ C. _____.

Step 3. Focus on subfear A. If rewriting this fear one more time seems unnecessary, note that the more you write about it, the more you diminish its power. With that understanding in mind, complete the following sentence now: "I am afraid that _____."

Step 4. Now, reread the subfear you described in Step 3 and ask yourself these two questions: (a) Are there any aspects of this situation that could be changed to make my partner safer or to improve my life? (b) Which aspects are beyond my control?

Step 5. While you're racking your brains thinking hard about these difficult questions, consult at least two other people. Each one must really care for you and your partner and be familiar with your personalities and the realities of your dilemma.

Step 6. Write down three aspects of this situation over which you do have some influence. (There may be fewer than three aspects. If you see no options, *do not* generate imaginary ones. Ask for feedback from others. If you still see no options, simply proceed to the next question.)

Step 7. Write down three aspects of this situation over which you have little or no control.

EXERCISE: Realistic Versus Unrealistic Options

This next exercise can help you sort out whether it makes sense for you to pursue any of the three positive options you identified in the previous exercise. Start a new page in your journal entitled "Realistic Versus Unrealistic Options" and follow the directions below:

Step 1. Select one of the three options you identified in Step 6 in the previous exercise and answer the following questions: (a) How much would pursuing this option benefit my partner and me? (b) Do I have the time, financial resources, stamina, and whatever else needed to follow through on this option? (c) Can I act on this option by myself or will I need the cooperation of others? (d) If I need help, which people and organizations can I trust to be reliable?

Step 2. After you have answered those questions, try answering these: (a) Do I really want to pursue this option or do I feel I *should*, perhaps because of others' expectations? (b) Would doing so run counter to my values or personality; would it create conflicts with important people in my life; or could it injure me, my partner, or others? (c) Will I be able to cope with the problems I've identified thus far and with other obstacles I might encounter?

Step 3. When you've finished answering the questions in Step 2 above, then tackle these questions: (a) How do the potential positive effects of pursuing this option compare to the possible negative effects? (b) Taking into account all the above considerations, to the best of my current knowledge, and after having discussed my plan with knowledgeable and caring others, is it wise for me to proceed? (c) If it makes sense to proceed, am I willing to develop a step-by-step action plan and follow through with it?

Step 4. If you've decided this option is simply not achievable or is not in your best interest, then return to Step 2 in "Identifying Options." Reread your subfear B and then examine it using Steps 1, 2, and 3 as outlined in this exercise.

Step 5. If you discover a workable option after examining subfear B, then go on to the following exercise. If you don't, return to Step 2 in "Identifying Options" above. Reread subfear C and examine it using Steps 1, 2, and 3 in this exercise.

Step 6. If you still haven't found an achievable option, don't give up hope. Consider consulting a mental health professional or some trusted friends. There may be options that you think are impossible that may be manageable with some planning and help from others.

EXERCISE: Action Plan

If you discovered a positive option, then proceed with this exercise. If you were unable to identify a positive option, then follow the suggestions in Step 6 above about consulting with a trained professional or trusted friends.

Start a new page in your journal entitled "Action Plan." Then answer the following question: In the previous exercise you identified a way to help ensure your partner's safety or improve your life that you decided would be both beneficial and feasible. What steps do you need to take to achieve your goal? Be as concrete as possible to describe these steps.

STRENGTHENING YOURSELF AND YOUR PARTNER

You and your partner can strengthen yourselves by improving the safety of your home and your workplaces and by taking care of your physical and emotional health. Although these steps may seem trivial compared to the dangers of living under the sword of Damocles, taking as much constructive action as you can will help ward off any preventable injuries and losses.

EXERCISE: Improve the Safety of Your Living and Work Environments

In this exercise, you will look for ways to improve the safety of your living environment. Start a new page in your journal entitled "Safer Living and Work Environments" and answer the following questions:

1. How safe is your home? Are there adequate locks and other safeguards on the windows and doors? Do you keep windows and doors locked at appropriate times? Are there any electrical or other structural problems, such as a leaky roof or a faulty gas heater? Do you have smoke alarms, carbon monoxide detectors, and fire extinguishers? Do you check them to be sure they are in working order? Are there any other safety problems in your home that need attention?

2. How could you make your home as safe as possible? Would it be helpful to join a neighborhood watch, get a dog, or get to know your neighbors better? If you live in an unsafe area, is it financially or otherwise possible to relocate to a safer area?

3. Is your car as safe as is possible? Is your insurance coverage adequate? Are the brakes, tires, and other parts in good working order? Do you use your seat belts faithfully?

4. Do you have photocopies of your credit cards, driver's license, bank account numbers, and other important financial and legal papers, in case the originals are lost or stolen?

5. Do you associate with people with histories of or tendencies toward violence? Do you walk in high-crime areas without taking proper precautions? If you can't stop these or any other behaviors that jeopardize your life, seek professional help immediately.

6. Do you live in a household or work in an environment that has guns, explosives, or other weapons? Are these weapons registered and securely locked? If you feel unsafe because of these weapons, are there any steps you can take to be safer?

7. Are you currently in a violent or abusive home or work situation? If the answer is yes, you need to seek professional care immediately. See appendix 2, Resources.

8. Would an exercise or weight-lifting program or a self-defense class increase your physical strength and confidence? Many people find that disciplined physical activity decreases their stress levels and increases their sense of control. However, it is mandatory that you get medical permission before enrolling in an exercise or self-defense program. It's also wise to check out the qualifications of the instructors.

9. Are you familiar with the safety codes of your workplace and those of your partner's? To what degree are these codes enforced? Are they observed by others? If not, why not? Do you and your partner observe these codes? If not, why not? Are the current codes adequate? Is there a formal process by which they can be evaluated and revised? If so, is it possible for you or your partner to become involved in this process? Is it practical for you to do so? What might be the emotional, financial, and other costs of your involvement? Do the possible benefits of altering the safety codes outweigh any emotional, financial, and other costs involved?

10.   Are there ways to improve safety on the job without changing
      the existing safety codes? For example, would it be helpful to
      take a class or learn more about aspects of your job? Are there
      items like computerized tools that would increase safety, yet not
      interfere with work performance? What would be the pluses and
      minuses of using a new method or item?

EXERCISE: Your Physical Health

Start a new page in your journal called "My Physical Health," and list
all of your medical concerns. Don't leave anything out, even problems
you think are "minor" or "all in your head." Consider all of the following recommendations:

Complete Physicals: If you haven't had a complete physical recently,
get one and find out when you will need one in the future.

Gynecological Visits: Because women's reproductive systems are
especially vulnerable to the effects of stress, regular gynecological
checkups, including Pap smears and mammograms, are essential.

Testing for STDs: If there is even a tiny possibility that you've
contracted a sexually transmitted disease (STD), get to a doctor or
clinic immediately. Be tested for chlamydia, gonorrhea, syphilis, her-
pes simplex virus, the HIV virus, and any other STDs your doctor
recommends. Don't procrastinate. Early treatment of an STD can
save your life.

Dental Visits: Letting your teeth deteriorate won't keep your
partner from harm. Untreated dental problems can lead to medical
problems elsewhere in your body. Review your list of medical concerns and prioritize them. (If possible, obtain medical help with this.)
Then, rewrite your list in rank order in your journal. Put the most
important medical concern first, and the least important, last. Leave
two or three lines between each entry.

Are you sure of the medical, dental, and other benefits provided
by your insurance plan? If not, ask for a complete list of benefits in
writing. Whether you have medical benefits through your partner's
work or have private insurance (or both), find the phone numbers of

the doctors or clinics you need for each condition. If you need to obtain a list of providers or authorization for a visit from your insurance company, do so. Inquire about coverage for physical therapy, medication, and alternative medicines.

If your health plan seems inadequate, find a better one. If you do not have insurance, call a local hospital, your county government, or local medical and dental schools for information on free or low-cost medical services.

Now, return to your journal and, for each medical concern, write the following: the names and phone numbers of the doctors or clinics you need to reach, the time period within which you will call for an appointment, the time period within which you will try to schedule an appointment, and your commitment to keeping the appointment. For example, "Medical issue #1: Dental work. Dr. Banks, phone number: _____. I will call the office by _____ (date) and try to make an appointment within _____ (specify time period). I commit to keeping this appointment." **Very important:** As soon as possible, ask a qualified medical professional to review your list of medical concerns. Based on their advice, you may need to reprioritize.

Your Partner's Physical Health

Your partner can work with the exercise above, "Your Physical Health," on his own. Even if he is eligible for medical services through his job, they may not cover all his medical concerns or, for any number of reasons, he may not have received them. If he is unwilling or unable to work with this exercise, you have the option to complete it in terms of what you know about his health. This suggestion is not intended to imply that you are responsible for his health.

You also can answer the questions in this exercise in terms of your children's health. If you aren't certain whether some of the symptoms you've observed in your partner or children are serious enough to warrant medical examination, don't make such decisions on your own. Even if you are a medical worker or are highly knowledgeable about medical matters, you still need to review your concerns with a medical specialist.

COPING SKILLS

By now, you might be asking yourself questions like these: "Suppose I do everything I can to strengthen my partner and myself and I complete all my action plans, and I'm still afraid? Suppose fear strikes me when I'm driving or when I don't have time to complete the recommended exercises? Suppose I go into a panic over those parts of my fears over which I have no control? How can I help myself then?"

Here, you will learn some ways to cope with such difficult situations. None of the suggested coping skills can eliminate your fears entirely. However, they can reduce the intensity of your fears, thus rendering them more manageable. Even a slight reduction in your fear level can make the difference between losing your emotional and mental control and having the ability to control your behavioral reaction to your fears.

For example, suppose news of an off-duty police officer being shot sends your heart rate soaring. Since your partner just telephoned you and you know he's safe, you tell yourself not to panic, but you panic anyway. You put the car keys in the freezer because your attention is a million miles away. You reassure yourself that you're not that upset, and then break a dish, yell at the mailman, and spill the garbage. When you find yourself standing in front of the refrigerator looking for something to eat even though you just ate, you finally admit you're beginning to lose control. At this point, using a coping skill can prevent you from doing more serious damage to your property or yourself. If you had used a coping skill after the first spike in your fear level didn't evaporate, you might have avoided spilling the garbage and the other minor mishaps.

If you use all the coping skills you learn from this book or other sources and you still find yourself trembling inside, don't become discouraged. If you were able to weather the storm of your fear without harming yourself, another person, or any other living being, you can consider yourself a success. The fact that you tried to help yourself rather than standing by helplessly while your fear threatened to engulf you is an affirmation of your inner strength.

Acceptance: Fear is exhausting; fighting it, even more exhausting. If there is one "rule" to observe, it's that fear is normal. If, you believe, on some level, that fear is a sign of cowardice, weakness, or mental ill-ness, then none of the methods in this or other books will be effective. If you continue to scold yourself for being afraid, you'll use up your valuable energy to undermine your self-confidence instead of applying it to manage your fears. Courage isn't so much the absence of fear, but trying—and notice I said "trying"—to maintain your integrity and act wisely in spite of your fear. A disabled combat veteran once told me, "Anyone who's stared death in the face and says he's never been afraid is a liar."

Riding Out the Fear: Some people find that if they let themselves experience their fear fully, without judging it or doing anything to make it go away, it sometimes it lifts on its own. But sitting with your fear until it subsides may not be an option for you. If riding your fear until it runs its course is intolerable for you, this doesn't mean you are a failure. If sitting it out is not an option, simply move on to any of the following coping skills.

Anxiety-Reduction Skills: When you are highly anxious, your ability to concentrate, think clearly, and exercise good judgment and other mental faculties can be significantly impaired. The self-calming skills described in chapter 1 are not problem-solving skills. However, by helping you to calm yourself, they can help restore your mental abilities.

Dialoguing: Are you angry with yourself that you are still afraid, even though you've already spent a lot of your valuable time working on your fears? Perhaps you want to punish the frightened part of yourself for feeling so helpless and confused? You must learn to acknowledge that your fearful self is still a part of your whole being. Pushing your frightened self away, fighting, or ridiculing her won't make her disap-pear; it will only use up psychic energy that you could be investing in your life today. If you really want to reduce the influence of your frightened self, you need to get to know her and make friends with her, no matter how much you despise her or wish she were different. You can build a relationship with her the same way you'd build a relationship with any other person: you talk to her and try to see things from her point of view.

One way to do this is to write a letter to her and have her write her reply to you. You may need to write many letters or find other ways to converse with her. If you see a therapist, Gestalt techniques, such as talking to parts of yourself during therapy sessions, might be very helpful.

EXERCISE: Write a Letter to Your Frightened Self

Step 1. A Letter to Your Frightened Self: Think back to a time when you were extremely afraid. Where were you? Were you alone or with others? What sensations did you experience in your body? What were your thoughts? What were your feelings? What did you do? With a picture of your frightened self in your mind, write a letter to her. For example, Maggie, a policeman's wife, wrote her first letter to her frightened self as follows:

> Dear You: I can't stand you. You're always thinking the worst. People are tired of listening to you, but no one is more sick of your hysterics than me. Other women are in your shoes, but they aren't such crybabies. You should be ashamed of yourself.

Step 2. The Frightened Self Replies: After you write the letter to your frightened self, have that part of yourself reply and continue the conversation. For example, Maggie's frightened self replied:

> Dear Maggie: Thanks for talking to me. I know I look like a monster and sometimes I act like a bully. But I'm here to help save your life, not destroy it. Just look past my scary face, and maybe I can help you.

Step 3. Dialoguing: To get the most out of this exercise, you need to maintain the dialogue between yourself and your frightened self. Write to each other as much as you can. For example, Maggie wrote the following letter back to her frightened self.

> Dear You: It just occurred to me that if you weren't so scary looking, I wouldn't pay any attention to you. If you looked normal, I'd probably just live my life, never giving a thought to preparing for disasters. But why do you have to come around just because you think something bad might happen? Can't you wait 'til you're sure it will? You've ruined so many good times with your stupid false alarms. Even if you are trying to be helpful, I hate you anyway.

By writing such letters, Maggie became more accepting of her frightened self and she used the energy she had spent loathing part of herself for better uses. If you can't complete these dialoguing exercises, then do some writing about why you can't. Also, discussing this issue with a qualified therapist is highly recommended.

THE FOUR-SENTENCE TECHNIQUE

When you're afraid, can you take a few moments to answer four short questions? A one-sentence reply to each is all that's needed. You can write your answers on paper, speak them aloud, or, if others are around, answer them in your head. This simple technique is especially useful when you need help immediately or you have very little time.

1. What is one (just one) of the fears you are experiencing right now? For example, "I am afraid that

   _____."

2. Look around you. Are you safe? If you aren't, get help. If you are, identify three or four objects in (or characteristics of) your physical environment.

3. How did you handle this or a similar type of fear in the past? (Remembering that you had the ability to manage your fear in the past and the specific ways you succeeded in managing it can help to restore your emotional stability.)

4. In spite of your fear, what can you do? (It's important to know that your fear hasn't stripped you of all your power and skills.)

Although you and your partner live under the sword of Damocles, you are not totally powerless. The coping skills described in this chapter can help prevent your fears from overwhelming you.

CHAPTER 5

Thinking the Unthinkable

No matter how much you prepare for the unthinkable—the death or disability of your partner—these are events for which you can never be truly prepared. It is impossible to predict the emotional impact of such devastating events. Also, your personality, financial and vocational status, interests, and family members will be different than they are today. Your local area, state, nation, and perhaps the world itself also may have changed, perhaps in ways none of us can even begin to imagine.

Nevertheless, as reluctant as you may be to think about losing your partner or seeing him maimed, for the sake of all involved, including your man, it is important to think about these dreaded possibilities as best you can. Although it is impossible to anticipate many of the challenges you will face, certain measures, in their limited ways, can help to minimize the emotional and financial disruptions that inevitably follow such a loss.

WHY IT'S HARD TO PREPARE

Most people find it extremely hard to think about death or disability. When they contemplate preparing for such events, they may tell themselves, "What's the rush? I'm probably not going to die tomorrow, so why ruin today?" For you and your partner, however, the possibility of harm doesn't lie in the distant future—it is an imminent reality.

This makes it even more important for you to prepare, yet it also makes it harder. This kind of planning isn't like making a budget; it can create conflicts within yourself and with others because it punctures the denial of death, a denial which you, your partner, and most of us need to keep on going. Also, you may not want to cloud whatever happiness you have in the present by preparing for tragedies. Yet you may be troubled already with anxieties about your future, and you know that, should the worst happen, being unprepared will only make your life that much harder.

It's also possible that you fear that talking or thinking about tragic events will cause them to happen. When for this, or any other reason, you hesitate to think about the unthinkable, keep in mind that even couples who don't live under the sword of Damocles write wills and purchase life, disability, and long-term care insurance. Even women whose men have relatively safe jobs worry about their future finances should their man be unexpectedly injured or killed. To prepare, they may begin thinking exploring their vocational and educational options.

How to Prepare

Various suggestions for preparing for your partner's premature death or disability are provided below. You can expect to feel sad as you work with them. If working with one of these suggestions is simply too heart wrenching or upsetting, stop your efforts immediately. You can always return to it to work on it later. The following suggestions are divided into two categories: practical considerations and emotional/social ones. These lists are not exhaustive. Therefore, it is highly recommended that you inquire about additional options by meeting with staff members at your personnel department, and any other professionals who might be helpful, for example, financial advisors, attorneys, or social workers at your local mental health facility.

You can avoid needless conflicts with your partner by obtaining as much information as possible about any areas of potential disagreement. For example, before you and your partner waste your time by disagreeing on funding your children's education, you need to be aware the full range of available educational opportunities and the financial options they may offer. If you anticipate conflicts about certain aspects of your will, you may need to consult with real estate agents, insurance representatives, stock brokers, attorneys, or spiritual advisors for more information. Second or third opinions may be also necessary.

If, however, your conflicts with your partner involve long-standing communication problems, resentments, or fundamental differences in personality or philosophies of life, professional help may be needed. A short-term round of couples counseling, focused specifically on resolving issues regarding preparing for the future and conducted by a trained mental health professional, or a spiritual advisor, may be helpful.

Practical and Financial Considerations

1. **Financial assets:** Compile a list of all assets, including bank accounts, stocks and bonds, insurance policies, retirement accounts, real estate properties, jewelry, vehicles, or other investments. Include any account numbers, contact numbers, and other relevant information.

2. **Survivor and disability benefits and medical and other insurance benefits:** Some of your most valuable assets may be any survivor and disability benefits available to you from your partner's employer; family leave or other assistance available from your employer; and benefits from any disability, medical, or other insurance policies you have purchased on your own.

You need to understand your coverage as much as possible. Reading the standard brochures about your coverage is seldom enough. Sometimes they are written in vague terms that don't specify exactly what you are entitled to, for how long, and under what conditions. Or they may contain confusing legal terms. Even when the information you have is clearly written, you will need to meet with a personnel or insurance representative or other informed responsible agent to answer your questions, and to obtain a clear understanding of the following:

The services or financial assistance to which you are entitled; the duration of the coverage for each different benefit; the claims process; any required documents other paperwork; any specific conditions you must meet before you can receive benefits; the expected time frame for receiving various benefits; any conditions under which your benefits could be increased, decreased, or revoked; and your options should you be denied some benefits or experience long delays or other problems in receiving them. If this information is absent in the official literature, ask for it to be put in writing and signed by an official with authority.

Don't forget to ask if there are code books, law books, or other legal documents regarding your coverage. Sometimes, these sources list additional benefits or specify certain restrictions or application procedures that are not described in the standard brochure. It is highly recommended that you meet with others who have gone through the process of applying for their benefits. They may have a wealth of information about dealing with any obstacles you may encounter.

3. **Financial liabilities:** Compile a list of your debts and other financial liabilities, including informal loans for which there is no paperwork. Your list should include contact information and account numbers or other relevant information.

4. **Wills:** You need to have two wills: one that describes the distribution of material possessions and another, a living will, that specifies preferences regarding life-support and for burial or cremation. Check with a reliable source to be certain that these wills are complete and in a form that will be acceptable in a court of law in your jurisdiction. Follow the procedures specified by your city, county, or state for registering your wills and for making them accessible to your executor and your heirs. Ask your partner for the names and addresses of any individuals whom you do not know that he would like you to contact in the event of his death.

5. **Important papers:** Safeguard important papers, such as passports, birth certificates, social security cards, court decrees, insurance policies, official paperwork, any other information about your assets and liabilities, copies of your will and your living will, any documents and other paperwork needed to claim benefits, and deeds to real estate or other property by placing them in a safe-deposit box or other secure location. Inform the executor of your will and a few trusted others about the location of these papers and provisions for access. Know the location of your income tax information and income tax returns.

6. **Legal matters:** Be aware of any pending lawsuits or claims. Ask your partner if he anticipates any legal matters or proceedings. Inquire also about past legal matters. Should they resurface, the more information you have about them directly from your partner, the better.

7. **Household, automobile, and other maintenance issues:** Someday you may be responsible for the maintenance of your property, such as vehicles, real estate holdings, appliances, works of art, computers, horses, or other livestock. You don't necessarily need to learn

how to do all the maintenance work yourself; but you do need to be familiar with the basic requirements of maintenance and know the location of any operating instructions, warranties, or other relevant information, and paperwork. Focus on those areas with which you are the least familiar. If your partner uses certain repairmen or companies, obtain their names and contact information.

8. **Additional preparations:** Even if you and your partner don't have rigid rules about who does what and you both share many responsibilities for your life together, in every couple and family there is usually some division of labor. Other than those tasks mentioned thus far in this book, what responsibilities do you tend to assume in the family? Which ones are generally the domain of your partner?

    Do some thinking about how you will handle functions formerly performed by your partner. For example, if your partner usually made the travel arrangements, did the grocery shopping, or maintained certain records, how might you be able to take care of these matters? Is it possible, or practical, that some of these functions could be delegated to another family member, even temporarily? Assuming you could afford to pay someone to take over some of these functions, would it be wise to do so? If there are responsibilities for which you need certain information and training, perhaps your partner, or another knowledgeable person, can advise you of available resources.

9. **Other sources of assistance:** Are there any financial, medical, counseling, educational, vocational, or other resources available to you through your local, county, or state government, or through the federal government? Does your community offer any financial assistance, for example, through food banks, clothing exchanges, and similar programs? Contact your local

social services department for information. Even if you don't anticipate needing this kind of help, knowing it is available can help to allay any fears of living in poverty.

10. **Employment:** If you are currently a homemaker or work part-time and you anticipate that your partner's death or disability would require you to assume a full-time job, don't panic. You don't need to line up a job or enroll in school or a training course tomorrow. You can, however, begin assessing your marketable skills and thinking about the types of jobs that would meet your needs.

You could find out about any vocational counseling services or job banks available in your area and make an appointment or two with a vocational counselor to discuss future possibilities. If some of the vocational options that interest you require additional education or training, you could begin researching the availability of this training and any available financial support. By taking these preliminary steps, if, someday, you need to begin working outside the home or find a higher paying job, you won't feel at a total loss as to how to proceed.

Personal and Family Considerations

1. Discuss your hopes for your children's future with your partner: their education, religious training (if any), and other important matters. If heated arguments result, you can call a time-out. Follow the suggestions in appendix 1, Guidelines for Effective Communication, for this and any other discussions about the difficult matters covered in this chapter. For example, if heated arguments arise due to the sensitive nature of these matters, you call a time-out.

2. Ask your partner what he would like you to remember about him: whether he has any important messages for certain people that he may not be able to deliver himself; and if he'd like to write letters to or make video- or audiotapes for you or other loved ones. You could even write letters or make tapes together. For example, Alicia and Joshua made an audiotape where they reminisced about some of the happiest—and funniest—events of their marriage. Listening to this tape after Joshua died was very painful for Alicia. Sometimes she couldn't bear to hear more than a few minutes of it. Other times, though, being reminded of the happy times in her marriage brought her some comfort.

3. Ask your partner if he'd like to share any stories about his family of origin, compile a family tree, or identify people in photographs whom you do not recognize.

4. You probably know a lot about your man. Yet there may be aspects of his life, personality, and beliefs with which you may not be familiar. Should you lose him, you may regret not knowing who his best friends were; the dreams he had for his life; or certain facts, like the schools he attended, his favorite hobbies and activities as a child and adolescent, the jobs he enjoyed, and his successes in life. If you already know the answers to these questions, you still may have other questions to ask him.

    Make it clear to him that this is not an interrogation: you aren't going to ask him to confess to wrongdoing, force him to disclose information he doesn't want to share, or bring up topics that you know or think might be painful or distasteful to him. If, inadvertently, you touch upon an area he doesn't want to discuss, he doesn't need to discuss it. He doesn't need to explain why he doesn't want to discuss it either.

Perhaps at some point in your relationship you may want to discuss some of your relationship conflicts. However, the purpose of this recommendation is not to bring up and try to resolve relationship problems. Your goal is to learn more about him so that you (and perhaps other loved ones) might feel closer to him not only in the event of his death, but in the present.

5. Discuss any issues pertaining to your families of origin, such as the care of family members who need special assistance or the handling of family members who have been problems in the past.

6. Do you have any unexpressed feelings of appreciation or affection for your partner that you would like to express? What way might work for you?

7. Do you and your partner spend quality time together? Before a particularly dangerous assignment or long separation, do you make an effort to spend time together just to enjoy each other's company? So many people lament the fact that they didn't set aside time for pleasurable experiences with their partner until it was too late.

    Together with your partner, make a list of ten or twelve activities that you would enjoy doing together. Don't screen out ideas that seem like impossible dreams. Review your list and ask yourselves, "Given our financial and other limitations, which of these activities could we realistically put into our lives?" For example, Joshua and Alicia loved lounging in bed listening to their favorite records. This cost nothing and only required them to rearrange their schedules.

    Then review your dream list. If your dream vacation is out of reach, is there a way to have part of it? For example, Joshua and Alicia wanted to take a vacation in Italy. There was no way they could afford that, but if they were careful with their money, they could dine out at Italian restaurants one or twice a month.

Talking about spending quality time together is much easier than actually doing so. For example, Joshua and Alicia's music time was constantly interrupted by other responsibilities and their Italian restaurant dates were often canceled because the money was needed for unexpected expenses.

However, when Joshua was promoted to a position involving more travel and more danger, Alicia insisted on following through with their plans on as regular a basis as possible:

"If I lose you, I want to have this time with you. Even if you're never hurt, we need this time for our relationship," she told Joshua. Several months later, Joshua lost his life on the job. Afterward Alicia said, "To think we worried about whether we could afford those Italian dinners or whether we could afford to take a few hours to listen to music and hold each other! How could we have afforded not to?"

8. Inquire about support groups or seminars on grieving and disability. There are also many helpful books on both of these subjects. (See appendix 2, Resources.) You don't need to attend a seminar or read one of the suggested books right now. In fact, you may never need or choose to do so. However, it can be reassuring to know that such support exists and is readily accessible should you ever need it.

9. Ask yourself the following questions: If I lose my partner, there will be a void in my life that nothing will ever fill. But as sad as I know I'll be, and I could be sad for a long time, what will be left? Who would I still care about and who would still care about me? Are there any activities that, down the line, after the shock of losing him subsides, that can somewhat provide me with some satisfaction and a sense of purpose?

Can I imagine finding some joy, however muted, in my work or in my relationships with family, friends, or others? Are there any people with whom I'd like to be closer? Are there any groups or organizations that could possibly offer me a sense of belonging or some safe companionship?

10. Identify your inner strengths. Ask yourself, "What can I count on within myself? Even if others fail me, what can I depend on inside myself to do or to be?"

11. Build on your strengths. Ask yourself, "How can I make myself stronger? What can I do to build on the strengths I have? Are there areas I could work on that would make me feel more competent or self-sufficient? For example, do I have any personal issues that may be blocking me from being my true self and developing my full potential? Would learning more about a certain subject or becoming adept at certain skills help me feel less afraid of managing without my partner? Do I wish to pursue any of these possibilities right now? If so, how realistic is it for me to try to do so?

"My fears about managing without my partner or coping with him becoming disabled may take their toll on me, and building on my strengths would help reduce these fears. However, my time and energy are limited. If I decide that making a commitment to expand one of my strengths would overtax me, thereby ultimately weakening me, that won't mean I'm lazy or not willing to try hard. It will mean just that I know my limits.

"If I choose to, I can review my options at some definite time in the future, for example, in a month or two, and at that time decide if I still want to act upon any of those options, and, if so, the feasibility of doing so. I might even have new ideas about what might help me by then. If I still feel it's not in my best interest to assume another commitment, I can set another date to revisit this decision."

In this chapter you learned about ways of preparing for the unthinkable: the injury or loss of your partner. Should the unthinkable occur, preparing for the future in these ways will spare you from the burden of having to cope with certain economic and practical matters. Being unprepared will only add to the emotional pain, fear, confusion, physical fatigue, and other reactions you are likely to experience after a tragic event.

Making advance preparations also permits your partner to participate fully in certain plans and decisions. This can bring you closer together. Furthermore, should the unthinkable occur, you will not have to wonder what he might have wanted or thought was best. You will already know. Also, you will probably feel more confident about some of your decisions knowing that you arrived at them together.

CHAPTER 6

Emotional Stress

The emotional stress of living under the sword of Damocles can lead to fatigue, forgetfulness, difficulties concentrating, irritability, slower reaction time, making errors even in routine tasks, and other stress reactions for both you and your partner. Emotional stress can also worsen any pre-existing health problems, harm your career, create serious relationship problems, and contribute to accidental injuries and deaths on the job.

Also, your partner's intimate acquaintance with death and dying can set the stage for the development of more severe problems, such as depression, post-traumatic stress disorder (PTSD), addictions (substance abuse, gambling, overspending, and sexual addictions), and other psychiatric disorders. In this chapter you will learn more about these disorders and how to develop ways to encourage your partner to seek help, should he need it. You may not be exposed to as many life-threatening situations as your partner, but your life contains so much uncertainty, stress, and long bouts of loneliness (see chapter 7) and sexual deprivation (see chapter 8), that you, too, may need to tend to your mental health and, if necessary, seek professional care.

DEPRESSION AND POST-TRAUMATIC STRESS DISORDER

Clinical depression and PTSD are common among those who work in dangerous occupations. The major symptoms of depression include hopelessness, fatigue, depressed mood; sleeping and eating problems; social withdrawal, memory and concentration problems; inability to experience pleasure; and thoughts of death or suicide.

Symptoms of PTSD include reliving traumatic events in the form of flashbacks, intrusive thoughts, sleep disturbances, nightmares, night terrors, hypervigilance (being constantly on the lookout for danger), and the startle response or jumpiness; numbing symptoms such as avoiding thinking or talking about life-threatening incidents on the job, or reminders of such incidents; feelings of impending doom; mood swings; and fears of mental instability, even insanity. Depression and PTSD are prevalent among men who were wounded or who blame themselves for the deaths or injuries of others.

As with physical problems, mental health problems are treated more successfully when treated early. Left untreated, they can damage a person's life and create or contribute to the development of serious medical problems or a life-threatening addiction.

ADDICTIONS: ALCOHOL, DRUGS, AND EATING DISORDERS

If your partner has an addiction, whether to alcohol, drugs, or gambling, he may be trying to numb himself. His addiction can consume so many of his waking hours that he doesn't have time to think about the dangers and human misery that surround him. Also, an addiction can be a form of self-medication for PTSD, depression, and anxiety attacks. Alcohol, certain drugs, and excess food, for example, help regulate sleep and suppress nightmares, reduce panic and anxiety attacks, and reduce despair and hopelessness, but only for a short time.

In the long run, however, addictions have a rebound effect and symptoms worsen. Almost inevitably, addictions lead to medical, financial, and relationship problems that aggravate any existing problems. Ironically, addictions can create the very problems they were intended to solve. Rarely do to they help anyone improve their self-esteem or cope with life's difficulties.

EXERCISE: Mental Health Concerns

Are you concerned about your partner's mental health? Do you suspect that his depressed mood, irritability and anger, mood swings, sleep difficulties, anxiety, cynicism, spending habits, sexual activities, or alcohol, drug, and food intake are interfering with his self-esteem, his work performance, his financial and physical security, or his relationship with you and with others? Do you have any similar concerns about yourself?

Now, on a new page in your journal entitled "Mental Health Concerns—My Partner" list the behaviors and attitudes you've observed in your partner that trouble you. On the next page write "My Mental Health Concerns," and list your own behaviors and attitudes that trouble you.

At your earliest opportunity, take these concerns to a trained mental health professional to determine whether you or your partner suffer from a condition that requires treatment, and for information on treatment options. Even if you have read extensively on various mental health problems and you own many self-help books, don't try to diagnose or treat yourself or your partner. Even doctors are not successful at healing themselves. (See appendix 2, Resources, for referrals to professional organizations.)

THE STIGMA OF MENTAL ILLNESS

To your partner, the suggestion that he may need psychological help may feel like a blow to his pride and sense of masculinity. In some instances, even the more socially acceptable suggestion that he needs to see a physician may be resisted. If this occurs, don't assume your partner is trying to act like a martyr. In dangerous occupations, unless a medical matter is urgent, it is sometimes seen as an unimportant issue compared to the need to get the job done. Furthermore, for your partner, taking sick time means leaving his team behind, which he may view as his "family." That is, your partner may have been trained to see his coworkers, especially those in his working group, as family members. In the military, a major goals of basic training is to create a team spirit that can overcome any racial, social class, or other differences.

"We watch each other's back," explained Jeremy. "Unless I'm really sick, I show up for work. If I'm not there, others have to pick up my load, which makes it harder for them to do their job. If they're overloaded, they might make mistakes and someone might get hurt. I'd rather be in pain all day long than have something like that on my conscience."

Some men hesitate to take sick leave for anything but the most pressing problems for fear of being viewed as slackers, sissies, softies, or cowards. Other men don't seek help thinking that they don't deserve it, because others are experiencing greater suffering. For example, Rob injured his back jumping out of a burning helicopter. "I had a lot of pain, but I told the medics I was fine. I didn't feel I had the right to complain—not when others around me were dying." Yet this incident put Rob in a wheelchair for life. Like Rob, Ben, whose job it was to identify body parts, refused needed medical care. "So I have a cancerous tumor on my neck? Big deal. At least I'm alive. The docs should be taking care of others, not me. At least I'm in one piece."

Whatever guilt and shame may exist regarding physical injuries and medical problems, they pale in comparison to the stigma of suffering from psychological stress. Despite progress in our current understanding of mental health problems, signs of psychological stress are still widely viewed as indications of moral, physical, or emotional inferiority, especially within the dangerous occupations. Your partner may fear, and justifiably so, that if his need for help were to be exposed, he would be seen as less competent or unfit for duty. As a result, he may try to hide his symptoms from his coworkers and his superiors and, perhaps, even from you. He even may have convinced himself that he doesn't have a problem, or if he does, that it is inconsequential.

EXERCISE: Encouraging Your Partner to Seek Help

Perhaps the most commonly asked question by women whose men work in dangerous occupations is this: "How can I get my partner to seek help?" In the final analysis, he is the only one who can decide that he needs help. He is not a child and, except in emergencies, you cannot force him to seek treatment. However, you can encourage him to seek help. Even if your efforts don't succeed, you will have the satisfaction of knowing that you tried your best to help him.

In this exercise you will develop some ways to encourage your partner to seek help that are suited to him as a unique individual. Although some suggestions will be provided, don't follow them blindly. As you read, think hard about your partner's personality and his work situation. You, not this author or others, are the expert on your partner. You know more than anyone else the approach that will be most effective with him.

Scolding him, telling him he is "crazy," or listing his character defects will not motivate him to seek help. It's also important not to approach him when he's tired, upset, restless, preoccupied with other matters, or while you are quarreling (or immediately afterward). It's also important to avoid using words or terms that might upset him. Try to follow the communication guidelines in appendix 1, and try to avoid repeating the same message of concern to him over and over again, for he will eventually grow immune to it.

Now, open a new page in your journal and call it "Encouraging My Partner to Seek Help." Follow the directions provided below and answer the following questions in your journal.

1. **Use, don't attack, his work values.**

    (a) What qualities does your partner value in himself or in others on the job?

    Before answering this question, take the time to recall instances when your partner expressed admiration for someone who displayed competence, dedication, or team spirit.

    (b) How might your partner's stress reactions interfere with his desire to live up to those values? Have there been instances when his symptoms interfered with his work performance? Note that if you know of a coworker whose symptoms did interfere with work performance, it may be easier to talk about the coworker's problems before discussing your partner's problems.

    (c) How can you express your concern that his symptoms could potentially harm a coworker (or someone he is trying to help) in a way that won't alienate him? Which words or phrases should you use? Which ones should you avoid?

    You may wish to point out the danger his symptoms pose to himself; however, he may have been trained to ignore or minimize such dangers. Therefore it's important to emphasize any specific ways his symptoms might be interfering with meeting his goal, instead of focusing on the goal of getting the job done with as few losses as possible.

    Although someone with a safe job might be able to get by with some of your partner's symptoms, his job requires a high degree of alertness. On slow days, his medical or psychological problems may not cause difficulties, but on stressful days, they can be troublesome. How would he feel if someone were injured or killed because he made a mistake caused by a physical or psychological problem? It is his duty to his team (as well as to you and others who love him) to maintain his emotional and physical health.

Similarly, if he suffers from overconfidence, he needs to learn to see refraining from unnecessary risk not as cowardice, but as emotional maturity and sound leadership. Sometimes, being told by a coworker that he's putting others at risk and compromising the mission by acting like a "rookie," a "cowboy," or a "know-it-all," can be extremely effective.

2.   **Address any fears your partner may have about seeking help that are based on myths.** Some widespread beliefs (or myths) hold that someone seeking mental health help is weak, unmanly, crazy, "psycho," or incompetent (as a person, family member, worker, or individual of faith).

   (a) Do you have reason to believe your partner has any of these fears? If so, which ones?

   (b) Do you have reason to believe that his coworkers, family, and others who matter to him believe in any of these myths? How is he affected by their views about seeking help?

   (c) Does your partner know of people who sought help and afterward were shamed, ridiculed, deemed unfit for duty, or even judged legally insane?

   (d) Are there any similarities between your partner's problems and his overall life situation and those of these other individuals?

   (e) What are the differences between your partner and these others? If your partner's symptoms are less severe than those of these others, or if his work, family, or financial situations are more favorable than those of these others, would it help to point out these differences to your partner?

- **Mental health problems are not all the same.** Although some people seek help for severe psychiatric illnesses, many seek help just for specific problems that affect only part—not all—of their life, or for problems caused by stressful situations, rather than anything related to their personalities. If your partner truly had a severe psychiatric problem, then he probably wouldn't be able to work or have a rational conversation with you. Unless he is out of touch with reality or in some way out of control, he can't legitimately be considered "crazy."

- **Mental health problems are often medical problems, too.** Inasmuch as the mind, body, and emotions are all closely interrelated, many psychological disorders involve various physiological abnormalities. Just as your partner probably wouldn't feel ashamed of having leukemia or diabetes, he needn't be ashamed of having a psychological disorder, because many psychological disorders have a physiological component. For example, alcoholism involves a biochemical addiction, and PTSD involves involuntary adrenaline surges and other physiological reactions. Similarly, depression can be caused by medical problems such as migraine headaches; low-grade neck, shoulder, or back pain; heart disease; diabetes; hypertension; chronic pain; cancer; and other long-term or life-threatening illnesses.

    Moreover, some physical illnesses, such as diabetes, hypoglycemia, hypertension, and urinary tract infections, have symptoms like irritability, emotional outbursts, and feelings of depression that appear to be psychological, but are really symptoms of a bodily illness. So, your partner may not have an emotional problem, but rather an illness that needs medical attention.

■ **Seeking help is a sign of intelligence, not weakness.** If your partner had a tool that needed repair, he'd be quick to fix the problem. He needs to see his stress reactions and other symptoms similarly. He would be foolish to ignore any symptoms or pretend that they will magically disappear. The sooner he acknowledges and finds ways to manage his symptoms, the sooner he will function at his maximum potential.

■ **Having stress-related psychological problems is not a sign of incompetence.** In fact, it is often a sign of the opposite. Frequently, it is the most competent, conscientious, and dedicated people who suffer from stress symptoms because they hold themselves to such high standards, or because they give so much of themselves to their work and families.

■ **Your man is not alone.** Many people working in dangerous environments develop stress-related symptoms and there are many books and articles that describe the effects of job-related stress on mental health. (See appendix 2, Resources.) Even those who don't work in dangerous occupations develop clinical depression, anxiety disorders, and other problems. According to a recent U.S. survey, between the years 1990 to 2000, approximately one out of every eight adults was using antidepressants (Langer 2000).

3. **Address any fears your partner may have that seeking help will mean he could lose control over his life.** For example, he may fear that he will have to comply with whatever a mental health professional may recommend; that he will have to attend months or even years of sessions; that he will be hospitalized or sent away to a rehabilitation center; or that he will be given psychiatric medications that will turn him into a "vegetable" or "zombie."

(a) Does your partner have any of the fears listed above? If so, which ones?

(b) Do you think your partner would benefit from you sharing any of these different perspectives on mental health with him? If so, which ones?

- **Seeking help isn't a lifetime commitment.** You aren't asking him to commit to decades of counseling. You are asking him to take two hours out of his life for an initial consultation with a trained professional, who may or may not recommend treatment. If treatment is recommended, many short-term treatments may be available. Suppose he is offered twelve two-hour sessions. You could say to him, "You owe yourself twenty-four hours of help. That's one day out of your life. Is that too much to ask for all the suffering you've been through?"

- **Unless he is suicidal or homicidal, or out of control in some way, he can't be forced to do anything against his will, much less be hospitalized without his consent.**

- **Your partner has choices.** Often several different treatments are available for a specific problem. He may be able to select the type of treatment he feels would suit him. If he is not given a choice, he can ask about options or seek a second opinion. Also, instead of seeing a mental health professional, he could read self-help and other books on specific problems; attend relevant classes or self-help groups; or talk to a clergyman or medical doctor about his concerns.

- **Should psychiatric medication be recommended, he can choose not to take it, or he may need to take it only for a short time.** Many people use psychiatric medication on a temporary, not a lifelong, basis to help them through a particularly rough period, and they never need to use it again. If your partner does take the medication and suffers unpleasant side effects, he can talk to his doctor about alternatives. In some instances, psychiatrists recommend relaxation techniques, energy therapies, therapeutic massage, acupuncture, improved nutrition, an exercise program, or other alternatives to psychiatric medications.

4. **Address any fears your partner may have that therapy is a waste of time.** If your partner believes that mental health treatment is useless, which, if any, of the following points of view and information might help persuade him otherwise?

    ■   Today there are many effective treatments available, especially for depression, anxiety disorders, and addictions. Some of these treatments are short-term and do not require in-depth analysis of personality. Many people in his field have benefited from such help.

    ■   Self-control, discipline, and personal power are important values in dangerous occupations. Treatment will strengthen, not weaken, him. Therapy is not a cure-all, but it can teach him how to manage his emotions so they don't run his life. He can learn more effective ways of dealing with people and with problem situations—all of which can boost his personal power.

    ■   You could also say to him, "Haven't you suffered enough? Don't you deserve a little help?" or "How do you know it won't help until you've tried?"

5. **Address any fears your partner has about his confidentiality being violated, or any other fears about speaking freely to counselors who are paid by his employer.** Unfortunately, there have been instances where confidentiality was violated, with negative consequences for the client. If your partner fears that

his confidentiality may be violated or if he believes that he can't speak freely to counselors paid by his employer, he can seek help outside the system.

Which, if any, of the following suggestions might be helpful? Rewrite the suggestions in your own words in a way that would best suit your partner.

- If he's entitled to mental health services as part of his job, you could say, "You're always complaining about how much is asked of you on the job. Well, here's a way your job can give something to you"; or "You're paying for these services; you might as well use them."

- If your partner refuses to seek help, ask him, "At what point would you decide you needed help?" In his opinion (not your opinion or a doctor's opinion), what thoughts or behaviors on his part would indicate to him beyond a doubt that it was time to see a mental health specialist? If he cannot answer this question for himself, ask him to answer this question in terms of yourself or someone else he loves: "What would you have to observe in me for you to decide that treatment was needed?" Similarly, with respect to overconfidence, you could ask him, "In your view, what's the difference between acting heroically and acting foolishly?"

- You can let your partner know that help is at hand by giving him the phone numbers of the mental health services available as part of his job and outside of his job. Also, you can give him pamphlets or educational materials about his condition and the available services.

- You may fear that if you push too hard, your partner will become even more resistant to the idea of seeking help. Perhaps you know better than even to mention the idea to him, knowing that it will be immediately rejected if it comes from you. If this is so, perhaps a respected coworker, friend, or member of the clergy might be more effective than you in convincing your partner that seeking help is an act of courage and honesty, not a sign if weakness.

MENTAL HEALTH EMERGENCIES

In some circumstances, you may not have the luxury of waiting for your partner to seek treatment. If he becomes so childlike, so violent, so self-destructive, or so disoriented that he cannot take care of himself or is a danger to himself or others, you may need to consider urging him to seek help and, in extreme cases, calling your local mental health department or emergency services for assistance. You may feel guilty about calling in rescue squads or literally driving your partner to a hospital or to an alcohol or drug treatment center for help. However, if he's having so much trouble functioning, you are not hurting or betraying him. You may save his life by forcing him to seek help. If he can't think or act rationally, you need to treat him as you would any family member who needs help, and you need to take control of the situation.

Some Final Words About Stress

In this chapter you learned about some of the emotional stresses of living under the sword of Damocles and about some of the common psychiatric disorders that can result from this stress. However, feeling emotionally stressed is not the same as suffering from a severe mental illness. Emotional stress, like physical illness, is a normal part of living. It's important not to confuse normal reactions to the many stresses in your life with the symptoms of a psychiatric disorder.

Don't assume that you (or your partner) have a serious mental disturbance just because you aren't happy most of the time, or because you have one or two symptoms of a psychiatric disorder described in this chapter. As a rule of thumb, you need to be concerned about symptoms when they result in self-harm or in harming others, or when they begin to interfere with the ability to meet responsibilities, to experience periods of contentment and joy, or to give and receive love.

Just as a minor cold doesn't develop into double pneumonia in a day, neither do signs of emotional stress develop into a psychiatric disorder overnight. As described in this chapter, there are warning signs that you can be alerted to in yourself or a family member. Should they become more frequent or more severe, you can take action to reverse the tide. (See appendix 1 for tips on effective communication and appendix 2 for other helpful resources.) By being informed and attentive to yourself and your family, you can help prevent emotional stress from robbing you of the life satisfactions you have worked so hard to attain.

CHAPTER 7

Loneliness

LONELINESS VERSUS SOLITUDE

We often feel lonely when we are alone, yet loneliness is not the same as solitude or the physical fact of being alone. Often we seek solitude as a healthy balance to our relationships, or for the opportunity to reflect upon our lives and connect with our feelings. One police officer's wife put it this way: "I'm more profoundly alone when no one is really listening to me or when I'm unable to tell my husband and friends how I really feel than when I'm literally all by myself." Loneliness is a part of everyone's life. However, for you, loneliness involves more than merely missing your partner when he's working long hours or working far away from home: it includes the fear that your current situation of loneliness might become permanent. This chapter explores some of our cultural attitudes toward loneliness, and the ways that loneliness can promote personal growth, as well as create self-doubts. Suggestions for coping with loneliness, especially on holidays and other special days, are also included.

CULTURAL ATTITUDES TOWARD LONELINESS

Unlike cultures in which marriages are dictated by custom, family ties, or economic necessity, Americans believe in love. Romeo and Juliet are our models for how couples are supposed to feel about each other. Their love was the be-all and end-all of their existence. You, too, may cherish your partner above all others, yet you also know that no one person can meet all of your needs.

However, as our society becomes increasingly mobile and our schedules increasingly crowded, our relationships with friends and family may suffer. In addition, certain aspects of your partner's occupation, for example, frequent relocations and long hours, can make it hard for you to make and keep close personal friends. Therefore, you may lack the caring relationships that might help to fill the void created by your partner's absence.

Even if you are fortunate enough to be surrounded by loving friends and family members, you may still experience the pangs of loneliness, for there are some needs that only your partner can fulfill. "When Dan's gone, I do all the right things: I call friends and catch upon on my reading, but that only goes so far," explains Diane. "I miss having someone to talk to about my day and to cuddle with at night. My friends love me, but I'm not their top priority, as I am to Dan. Sometimes, when I see couples holding hands, it's hard to hold back my tears."

Although loneliness is a normal part of the human condition, Diane often feels ashamed about her feelings of loneliness. "I can understand feeling lonely when Dan is gone for weeks or months, but not when he's away because of an emergency," Diane said, failing to see that missing someone, even if he's gone only for a few hours more than usual, is a natural part of loving that person. But Diane fears that if her feelings of loneliness are more intense or long lasting than others deem acceptable, she will be seen as weak or self-centered.

For example, she has been told: "There's no reason to be that lonely. Grow up! Nobody should need another person that much! He'll be back in a few weeks. Even if it's longer, it's not forever." Because of such attitudes, Diane doesn't discuss her painful loneliness with others. She even protects Dan from the full extent of her misery. "I want him to know I miss him, but he's got enough to worry about without having to worry about my unhappiness," she explains.

In her efforts to "adjust faster" to Dan's absence, Diane reads articles in women's magazines on how to have a fulfilling life without a partner and she follows their suggestions. Yet all her efforts provide only temporary relief, thus confirming her belief that she is inadequate because she isn't "back to normal" within a week, as the magazines say she could be, if only she tried harder.

Unfortunately, Diane isn't aware of the power of *mood-dependent memory*. That is, when we are in a certain mood, we tend to recall experiences when we were in the same mood (Meyers 2002). As such past memories arise, our current mood is prolonged and may even intensify. Because your moods affect your thoughts, your mood at the moment affects your perception of yourself, others, your current life, and your future.

For example, if you are feeling self-confident, unless there is an interference with your mood-dependent memory, you will tend to recall earlier instances when you felt good about yourself. Because of these positive memories, you will continue to feel self-confident. Your self-esteem may even rise. Your view of your life today and of your future will be optimistic. In contrast, feeling lonely will remind you of other lonely times, making you feel even lonelier. Life today will seem forlorn and empty, and your future, dark and loveless.

Whenever Diane passes Dan's closet, she starts to cry and feels like a failure. When her loneliness subsides a bit, she wonders if this means her love for Dan has lessened. So do others. Diane says, "When I'm fine, and many times I am fine, I'm told it's unnatural for a woman not to miss the man she loves." Yet it is entirely normal for loneliness to lessen as one adjusts to being alone; loneliness, like any other feeling, tends to vary in its intensity. The human psyche cannot tolerate extreme emotional suffering indefinitely. Just as ongoing physical pain can lead to a state of shock where one feels little or no pain, emotional shutdown can follow intense emotional pain.

Juliet Versus the Iron Woman: During Dan's absences, Diane must cope not only with her loneliness, but also with her guilt and the self-doubts created by a cultural double bind that affects many women.

On the one hand, she is expected (and to some degree expects herself) to be like Juliet, who can't imagine being happy without Romeo at her side. On the other hand, she is expected (and to some degree expects herself) to be an Iron Woman who prevents herself from feeling her own feelings in order to withstand the tensions created by living under the sword of Damocles.

The Iron Woman strives to maintain her partner's morale by keeping the home fires burning and providing him with whatever support she can. It is also her role to encourage him to "be tough" and help him to focus on the importance of his work. Complaining and "being emotional" are taboo: they distract him from his duties and could result in an accident. She seldom weeps, even in the privacy of her home. In contrast, Juliet openly laments being apart from Romeo and doesn't hesitate to tell him—or the world—how much she needs him.

In general, our society honors the self-sufficiency displayed by Iron Women. Independence is seen as a sign of strength; dependency, a sign of weakness. If Juliet were alive now, some would see her as a "needy," woman who "loves too much." Yet no one is totally independent and no one (except for very young children) is totally dependent. Mental health requires a balance of both.

Opportunities for Personal Growth: Existential Loneliness

Much of Diane's life was structured by the needs and patterns of her relationship with Dan. When he left, he took part of the structure of her life and part of her identity with him, leaving a vacuum. In encountering this vacuum, Diane also confronted her existential aloneness: the knowledge that she was born alone and would die alone, and that she was essentially alone with her decisions and their consequences. She asked herself, "What really matters to me?" The answers didn't come easy, plummeting her into anxiety and confusion.

Realizing there are no guarantees, she decided to take a chance on something small and enrolled in a cake-decorating class. Although not intending to become a full-time baker, the praise she received from her classmates boosted her self-esteem. Also, she was proud of herself for doing something constructive to combat her loneliness and not running from it, as she had in the past. The class also helped ease her loneliness. At least one night a week, she spent time with others.

However, like many women, Diane had mixed feelings about her growing self-confidence. She says, "The first few separations from Dan were hard, but I did stuff that helped me feel less lonely, and I grew stronger. Now I don't dread being separated the way I used to, and he's relieved because I'm happier. But we both worry about growing apart. It's hard enough when he leaves, but sometimes he comes back changed, and if I start changing, too, can our love survive?"

Loneliness, Anger, and Grief

Before a scheduled workweek involving longer or more inconvenient hours or an out-of-town assignment, you and your partner might wish to cherish every moment of your remaining time together. However, instead of acting like Romeo and Juliet, you may find yourselves feeling angry—or distant—from one another. Either you, your partner, or the two of you may become more irritable and look for any excuse to start a heated dispute.

You may be confused as to how you can feel sad about your partner's leaving, even to the point of tears, and then start feeling hostile or emotionally numb toward him. He may be similarly bewildered by a roller coaster of emotions for you. Yet, there are valid reasons for these unromantic but quite common emotional patterns.

The sheer strain of taking care of any necessary logistical changes can lead to physical and psychological overload. Often there is little time to get in touch with one's feelings or to share quality moments with one's partner. Under such conditions, as would be expected, increased disagreements, if not outbursts of anger, can easily follow.

The most profound source of the increased strain in your relationship, however, is not the hassle of rearranging certain details of your life. Rather it is the awareness of impending loss—the realization that soon you will have less time together and be without the emotional and physical security of having your partner nearby. Anger is part of the grieving process and can express the underlying sense of loss or the anticipation of loss.

Anger and faultfinding also can be ways to separate oneself from another person to lessen the pain of missing that person. Anger is also a way to express feelings of powerlessness and fear. If the upcoming changes put your partner at greater risk, his anger, like yours, may be a reaction to the increased danger. Suppressing the anger can lead to numbing, which further strains your relationship, as does expressing anger through emotional and sexual withdrawal.

Loneliness: Separating Past from Present

Due to the power of mood-dependent memory discussed above, feeling lonely in the present may bring up memories of past lonely times. Hence, some of the thoughts and feelings you are experiencing currently regarding your partner's absence may belong to previous lonely times. For example, suppose you felt lonely after a man you loved left you because he thought you weighed too much. As result, in the present, you could be burdened not only with the loneliness of your partner's absence, but with doubts about your attractiveness related to your past.

Your current situation is painful enough without the extra burden of experiencing unhappy feelings that belong to the past. The following exercise can help you separate your current situation from earlier experiences of loneliness. Be sure to complete this exercise if you have been rejected, abandoned, or mistreated by others, especially during your childhood.

EXERCISE: Loneliness—Separating Present from Past Situations

Start a new page in your journal labeled "Loneliness—Separating Present from Past Situations," and briefly describe a time in your past when you were extremely lonely or when you were rejected or abused by someone you loved or upon whom you were emotionally or financially dependent. Do not ignore a situation because you, or others, believe that your memory is distorted or that you are exaggerating your pain.

In your journal, answer the following questions: "What are the similarities between this past circumstance and my current one? What are the differences?"

In answering these questions be as specific as possible. Identify concrete similarities and differences between your present situation and your past experience of loneliness or, if relevant, between your partner and the person who deserted you in the past. Also consider the similarities and differences in terms of your personal strengths, your relationships, your financial and educational status, your health, and any other relevant factors. If you choose to, you can use these questions to examine any further instances of loneliness.

This is how Becky completed this exercise:

Past lonely experience: When my ex-husband went on long business trips, he'd ask me to contact him daily, but then he complained that I was "too needy." He left on a business trip right after my brother died, even though the trip could have been postponed. When I had problems, sometimes he was supportive but other times he accused me of "whining." After six years of marriage, he said that the main reason he went on these trips was to get away from me.

Current situation: My boyfriend Tom was overseas for a year and is now on a six-month assignment nine hundred miles from home.

Similarities: Doesn't keep in touch as much as I do; secretive about their work; want me to "be strong" and do things for them while they're gone (like call their mothers and send them brownies); say they love me; give me short notice about when they're leaving; both are good-looking; both, to the best of my knowledge, were sexually faithful.

Differences: Tom contacts me more frequently than my ex; Tom doesn't talk about work due to security reasons, my ex because he wanted to shut me out; I've visited Tom twice, my ex never let me visit him; Tom has never ridiculed me for missing him. Today, I'm more emotionally mature, make more money, have more friends and a stronger faith. But I'm more anxious about getting pregnant because I'm older.

After completing this exercise Becky wrote: "When Tom was away, I used to panic because I was afraid that, like my ex, he didn't really love me. Writing down the ways that Tom is different from my ex gives me concrete evidence that, so far, my trust in Tom is not wishful thinking. Also, itemizing how I have changed since my divorce helped me be less afraid of being alone again. I have more going for me now than I did back then."

If, after completing this exercise, you are still troubled by feelings that, in your view, have more to do with your past than your present, seek professional care.

COPING WITH LONELINESS

The coping techniques provided in this section cannot eliminate all of your loneliness. They can, however, help you find ways to treat yourself as lovingly and respectfully as possible during your lonely times, ways to use loneliness constructively, and ways to comfort yourself, or allow others to do so. Every time you realize you have constructive ways to help yourself feel better, you will grow stronger and more courageous.

Experiment with the various techniques described below until you find some that work for you. Note that an idea that works one time may not work the next. If a certain technique isn't helping, go on to another coping skill. If none work, you simply will need to ride out the loneliness, frequently reminding yourself that so long as you do not harm yourself or anyone else, you are a success.

1. **Respect your loneliness, don't fight or deny it.** If you want to feel less lonely, the first step is to accept your loneliness. You will never be able to lift your mood if

you are spending your energy fighting it or holding it down.

2. **Remember the people who care about you.** Feeling lonely doesn't mean no one cares about you. Think about it: Do you care about people who are elsewhere or whom you haven't contacted recently? Suppose some of them concluded that because you weren't in the same room with them or because you hadn't contacted them lately, that, therefore, you had little or no genuine concern for them. What might you say to those people? Most likely you'd assure the individual that he or she was important to you. Remember to give yourself the same message when you feel abandoned and unloved.

3. **Make a mental list of people who have shown you love or concern over the past few years or write their names in your journal.** Reminding yourself of these people can help you to feel less lonely. Contacting them may help even more.

4. **Do not expect your mood to be stable.** Loneliness can involve emotional numbing as well as emotional pain; apathy as well as the energy for a flurry of activities; and a desperate need to be with others, as well as a profound need to be alone. At times, you may find yourself becoming more sensitive to rejection or criticisms (real or perceived). Other times, however, you may find yourself becoming "hardened" as a form of self-protection against the pain of loneliness or against the impersonal or hostile treatment of others.

5. **Find ways to express your loneliness.** Don't carry your loneliness as a psychological or medical symptom. Take the time to write about it in some depth or to express it in music, art, or dance. You don't have to be dramatic, or public, about how you express your

loneliness. For example, you could take a few moments to think about your partner or reminisce about positive times together; or write down "I miss you" or "I'm lonely right now" on a piece of paper.

If expressing your feelings is difficult for you, don't force yourself to do it. Let others do it for you. There is no lack of music, media programs, novels, and other literature about missing a loved one or feeling lonely. Ask your local librarian for assistance in locating materials on this topic. Some of the suggestions in the section "Emotional Needs" in chapter 8 also may prove helpful.

6. **Lower your expectations, temporarily, until you've had the necessary time and gathered the necessary supports to adjust to your partner's absence.** When you are feeling particularly lonely, you may experience fatigue and memory or concentration problems. Just as you would not expect yourself to function at an optimal level while physically ill, you cannot expect yourself to be as efficient and productive as you were when your partner was with you. Temporarily, your life will not be as balanced because loneliness turns your energies inward, not outward, especially on holidays or other special days.

Identify your essential responsibilities and then be willing to let go of all the rest.

7. **Make plans.** Certain creative, spiritual, and other efforts require large blocks of unstructured time. In general, however, long stretches of unstructured time set the stage for feelings of loneliness and despair. Without overscheduling yourself, try to schedule some meaningful, pleasurable, or social activity into each day, especially on weekends or other times that you usually spent with your partner. You may not be able to follow a specific plan exactly, but it's important to have one.

8. **Maintain and increase your connections with others.** At times, you may need to withdraw from others in order to experience your feelings in the privacy of your home. However, it is critical that you stay connected with supportive others. You also can try to expand your network of friends by meeting new people. If you've always wanted to join a hiking group or become more active in a community, school, or volunteer organization, or within your community of faith, this might be a good time to pursue these possibilities. Your partner's employers may provide support groups for partners. (See appendix 2, Resources.) Perhaps you could find comfort in having a pet. Avoid spending time with critical others.

9. **Stay connected to your loved one.** General feelings of loneliness can be eased by contact with others, but your specific loneliness for your partner can be eased only by contact with him. Letters, e-mails, phone calls, care packages, audio- and videotaped messages are the most obvious ways of staying connected. Allow yourself to write as many letters, prepare as many gifts, and so forth, as you wish. If it is necessary for you to limit your contact, you can continue to write him letters but not send them.

   Additional suggestions include these: look at photographs; create photo albums; read old love letters; write about or record stories about how you met or about any humorous, romantic, or important events in your life together; go to places you used to frequent together; keep in touch with his family and friends; talk about him to others; carry a photograph of him or a small object that reminds you of him in your purse; imitate his positive behaviors, such as his participation in a charitable effort; learn more about his work or his current geographical location; read books that he's read or watch movies he's seen so you can discuss them later; or become involved in or initiate an effort to contribute to his occupation. If you are spiritually inclined, you could pray for your partner or arrange a special service for him.

Unhealthy ways of dealing with loneliness include self-harm (such as smoking, overspending, cutting yourself, or abusing liquor or drugs); self-deprivation (such as denying yourself needed medical or psychiatric care, healthy companionship, or fun); repeatedly berating yourself for making certain mistakes or for not being perfect in some area; imitating your partner's negative behaviors (for example, overeating because he overate, or becoming angry in certain circumstances because he became angry in these particular situations); or taking on his guilt for a particular matter even though you were not involved. None of these efforts to feel closer to your partner have the power to make him safer or to bring him back any faster.

10. **Reexamine your priorities to find ways to use your loneliness for positive change.** Your partner's absence may give you more time for home projects, reading, gardening, or other such endeavors. Consider also the following two exercises developed by Julia Cameron (1992):

- **Uncovering buried dreams:** Think about hobbies and classes that sound like fun; "things you used to enjoy doing;" and "silly things you'd like to try once" (Cameron 1992, p. 86).

- **Time travel:** "Describe yourself at eighty. What did you do after fifty that you enjoyed? Be very specific. Now, write a letter from you at eighty to you at your current age. What would you tell yourself? What dreams would you encourage?" (Cameron 1992, p. 89).

11. **Prepare for predictable hard times, such as birth-days, holidays, and other special days.** You can expect to feel especially lonely for your partner on special days (such as birthdays and holidays) or at certain times during the week you usually were together, or which couples generally spend together (like weekends). At these times, you may need to try several of the methods described above, and it is critical that you make specific plans that include some form of personal human contact. You need not talk about your loneliness or your partner. You might simply ask a relative or friend go for a walk or have a meal with you. Telephone calls, e-mails, or letter writing are also useful, but it's best to spend time in the actual presence of another person.

At family gatherings, if you wish, you can acknowledge your partner's absence publicly. Those present can join in writing messages to him on a card or in a letter or in preparing an audio- or videotape to send to him. Another possibility is for others to share a positive memory about him or the ways they cope with missing him. You can also ask other women how they cope with these difficult days. If all else fails, do something nice for someone else. Doing good deeds for others is a surefire way to take your mind off your troubles.

CHAPTER 8

Sex and Sexual Jealousy

Author's note: The purpose of this chapter is to describe some of the sexual struggles confronting couples who live under the sword of Damocles, not to promote or critique any particular religious or philosophical views of human sexuality. Skip any parts that make you uncomfortable. If you choose, you can skip the entire chapter and still benefit from this book. Remember, the suggestions offered here are just that: suggestions. You and your partner are the experts on each other, and the two of you will work out how best to deal with your sexual concerns.

All couples struggle with a variety of sexual issues, but this chapter focuses on four concerns specifically related to your partner's occupation: sexual disinterest, sexual urgency, sexual deprivation, and sexual jealousy. Either you, your partner, or both of you may be troubled by one or more of these and perhaps additional sexual concerns as well.

The first step in coping with any sexual concern is to get a thorough medical exam. Because most sexual problems are rooted in personal or relationship issues, a close look at your satisfaction with yourself and with your relationships (not only with your partner, but with others) is also in order. It's also important to learn more about human sexuality in general and your sexual concerns in particular or to consult with a qualified sex therapist.

SEX IS MORE THAN SEX

Sex is more than a physical means of releasing tension: it is also a way of communicating affection and love. In our society, sex is often reduced to genital contact, and a heavy emphasis is put on achieving orgasm, rather than on experiencing the emotional warmth and intimacy that sex can foster. To the extent that sex is orgasm-focused, it becomes more like work than play.

Sex and Stress

Each woman is unique. In sexual matters, especially, there is wide variability. Some of you may believe in monogamy so deeply that thoughts of infidelity would never cross your mind. Some of you are physically faithful but also troubled by sexual temptation. Still other women may have broken their promises of fidelity or may believe in sexually open relationships.

Women also vary in the strength of their desire. Some women have stronger sex drives than others. However, every woman's desire is influenced by the quality of the nonsexual aspects of her relationship with her partner. Although society gives men greater permission to separate sex from their emotions, their sexuality too can be profoundly influenced by relationship problems. In our fast-paced society, even couples in safer circumstances than yours frequently discover that their many commitments drain them of sexual energy. Sometimes, what begins as a week or two of not touching can extend to longer periods. For the two of you, all these average, everyday problems are heightened by the fact that you live under the sword of Damocles.

On the other hand, your mutual awareness of the fragility of life can lead to a stronger determination to cherish one another, not only in bed, but in all the other parts of your relationship, too. Sue explains: "Having seen death up close, my husband now appreciates life in a way that someone who is still in denial about death cannot. He values his job and family far more than he does appearances or material objects. Sexually, he's unbelievably tender."

SEXUAL DISINTEREST

Exposure to death and dying can dampen the sex drive of most men. The psychic numbing that often develops under conditions of extreme stress can leave your man feeling not only emotionally "empty," but sexually inert as well. You may be similarly troubled. Even if your partner doesn't talk much about his work, the media provides you with plenty of pictures of the most tragic aspects of his job. It's hard to feel sexy when thinking of matters like these.

Some men experience periods of sexual disinterest due to particularly stressful experiences on the job. But with a little time to recuperate, their sexual functioning returns to normal. Similarly, you may have little interest in sex after a really hard day or after becoming aware of the tragedies your partner has encountered. But with time to rejuvenate yourself, your interest is likely to return. If it doesn't, you may need to consider other factors that have been found to diminish sexual interest and performance: inadequate rest and exercise; medical problems; financial stress; aging; certain medications; loss of a loved one; relationship conflicts; alcohol, drug, or food addictions; and the impact of traumatic incidents unrelated to your partner's work.

Coping with Sexual Disinterest

If either you or your partner shuts down sexually, the first step is to be honest about it. In our sex-obsessed culture where sexual

disinterest is often seen as a sign of failure, admitting to sexual disinterest is not easy. But keeping it a secret or making excuses, like having a headache, solves nothing. In contrast, a clear statement like
"My feelings for you haven't changed one bit, but I'm not feeling sexual right now (or lately)," can be freeing.

If you wish, you can refer to the specific incident that has
affected you. Refrain, however, from graphic descriptions of human
suffering that could retraumatize either or both of you, which could
lead to even more sexual shutdown, or the opposite, increased sexual
desire. Follow the communications guidelines about discussing painful
topics provided in appendix 1.

For example, even if your mind is preoccupied with horrible
images, don't say to your partner, "When you kiss me, I see the blood
running down the legs of the rape victim you helped today." All you
need to say is, "Rape is so depressing; it's hard for me to feel sexual."
If you need to talk about a horrible event in detail, do so with a
trained therapist, not your partner.

In addition, be sure to speak of the positives: that you cherish
being with him; that shut-down feelings don't last forever; that sharing sadness can bring you closer. For example, you could say, "I want
to be close to you, but right now I can't stop thinking about some of
the awful things you see at work. When the sadness lifts, I know I'll
want to be with you more fully." If you wish, you can suggest a
nonsexual form of touching, such as "I'd like it if you'd hold my
hand" (or "put your arms around me"). Encourage your partner to be
honest too, emphasizing this doesn't mean he has to explain himself
or describe a horrible event. Tell him that a simple statement, like "I
feel bad because something bad happened today," is enough.

Scheduling Sex

Long hours, busy lives, and the many emergencies that are part
of your life make it important for the two of you to consider scheduling sex. The schedule can be fairly informal, more like a simple
understanding that you will try to have some private time together
regularly. Scheduling sex may not sound romantic, but it can keep
not having sex from becoming a "habit."

Reserve the Bedroom for Lovemaking and Sleep

In general, it's best to reserve the bedroom for sleep, lovemaking, and other pleasant activities. It's not a good idea to keep a television set or a computer in the bedroom.

SEXUAL URGENCY

Living under the sword of Damocles can also increase sexual needs. For some, this increase may reflect stress-related increases in adrenaline and blood flow. For others, there may be an urgent quality to sexual desire that cannot be attributed solely to the need for sexual gratification. From time to time, both men and women have found themselves wondering if their partner is seeking not only sexual release, but also security and self-esteem. They also may wonder whether their partner is using sex to increase emotional closeness or its opposite, that is, to gloss over relationship problems. Or they may be concerned that their partner is using sex as a "tranquilizer" for emotional pain, anxiety, anger, and other powerful and troublesome emotions.

Using sex to relieve tension is not necessarily unhealthy: one valuable biological effect of sex is physical relaxation. But when one partner uses sex to cope with stress so that sexual activities feel mechanical and devoid of affection, one or both of the partners can lose interest.

Problems also arise when sex is used for purposes for which it was not intended, such as a solution to family problems. Sex may provide temporary relief, but it is not a long-term solution for these or for similar problems. Other approaches will be needed.

Increased sexual desire is to be expected at particularly stressful times, with a return to more usual levels after the stress has subsided. However, if either you or your partner find that your need for sex as a tranquilizer hasn't decreased or is causing relationship or other problems, you will need to evaluate your situation and find other ways to manage your stress.

SEXUAL DEPRIVATION

Under conditions of sexual deprivation, it is normal for sexual desire to increase, decrease, remain the same, or alternate between the three possibilities. A pattern may evolve or there may be no pattern. You may react the same way each time your partner is away, or your reaction may vary from one separation to the next. Try not to judge your body's response to sexual deprivation. For some women, sexual interest seems almost to disappear. (This may happen even before their partner departs.) Rather than endure sexual frustration, your body puts your sex drive on hold. Moreover, when your partner is away, you also must deal with fears about his safety, added responsibilities, and perhaps children who miss their father.

Any one of these stressors alone could dampen the sexual interest of most women and could affect their hormonal balance, menstrual cycles, and other aspects of their gynecological health, as well.

A diminished sense of desire is not always cause for alarm. Unless you encounter major nonsexual problems that need attention, your natural sensuality most likely will reemerge once your partner has safely returned. But an adjustment period may be needed. Our bodies are not machines. They don't turn "on and off" on command. If you have concerns about your sexual functioning, consult a gynecologist or a qualified sex therapist. (See appendix 2.)

Women and Shame: Sexual Dreams and Thoughts

Some women panic when their sex drive diminishes, others are relieved. Some wish they could put sexual need on the back burner, but it keeps emerging, creating both physical and emotional distress. Every time a woman's body hungers for its mate, she may be reminded of his absence and the loneliness and many fears that go along with it. Sexual deprivation may lead to an increase in sexual dreams and thoughts. Don't be overly concerned about such dreams. Just as hungry people dream about food, these dreams can be your psyche's way to compensate for the lack of sexual activity in your life.

Historically, women have been taught to feel ashamed of their sexuality. Even today, despite the advances in women's rights and the media glorification of female hypersexuality, women often experience a sense of shame about their sexuality. But having sexual thoughts or dreams is not the same as acting on them. Women often focus on the fact that they had a sexual thought or dream and disregard the fact that they remained loyal.

Furthermore, some people are unfaithful even when their partners are close by. Women who remain true, even when their sexual needs are not being met, demonstrate a high degree of self-discipline and dedication, regardless of their dreams. For some of you, however, having sexual thoughts or dreams is just as unacceptable as acting on them. Nevertheless, the fact that your behavior conforms to your beliefs deserves recognition.

SEX, AFFECTION, AND GRATITUDE

For many women, affection and sexuality are so closely connected that they may confuse their affection for someone who offers them support during their partner's absence with being sexually interested in that person. However, upon closer examination, most women realize their interest in this kind person is emotional, not physical. If sexual feelings do develop in either the woman or the man, clear boundaries must be set. Such situations can be very delicate and you may need the guidance of wise and trusted friends or a qualified mental health professional.

Unscrupulous Men

You may be approached by a man who, under the guise of offering you support, tries to take sexual or economic advantage of you. Such men are often charming. Thus, it's easy to be drawn into an innocent friendship, only to have him try to introduce a sexual element. Even if you withdrew from him the minute you saw through his façade, and even though he, not you, was seeking an illicit relationship, you may continue to suffer from guilt and shame.

Don't take responsibility for the behavior of an unscrupulous person. It was not your loneliness, attractiveness, or "sexual vibe" that "lured" him to your side. From ancient times to the present day, there have always been men who try to exploit the emotional and sexual vulnerability of women whose men are away at war.

COPING WITH SEXUAL DEPRIVATION

Lack of sex doesn't have to mean lack of fun, lack of pleasure, or doing without the presence of someone who cares about you. Some of the nonsexual needs met during intimacy can be satisfied—at least in part—with safe nonsexual behaviors. The coping methods described here cannot eliminate your longings for your partner, but they can lessen their intensity.

Emotional Needs

Listed below are some emotional needs that women find to be important aspects of intimacy, and some of the safe ways they try to meet those needs when their partner is away.

Being the sole focus of someone's attention. "During sex, I had the undivided attention of someone who cares about me. To get that when my boyfriend is gone, I meet with a friend or a relative one-on-one in a quiet place. I try to make myself the focus of my attention, too, by thinking about my needs and feelings.

Feeling like a woman. "I refuse to look dumpy! I do things that make me feel feminine even if it's putting on makeup at home rather than in the car during red lights. But I stop my efforts when they stop feeling like fun or when I start feeling inferior to supermodels."

Feeling special—feeling loved. "Buying myself a single rose can go a long way toward making me feel special. Every day I try to do something for myself, even if it's just spending a little more time in the shower. That might not sound like much, but with three children and a full-time job, any time spent on myself that lasts longer than five minutes feels like a vacation."

Giving love. "I try to show more love to the people I already love, and I look for new people to care about, too. There's always a neighbor, relative, or coworker whom I can get to know better. And suddenly my world becomes a more loving place."

Playing, taking a break. "I look for small bits of time when I can do something, anything—as long as it's not remotely connected to work—like taking ten minutes to listen to music or stopping at a yard sale. I still miss my husband, but I don't feel like such a martyr."

Some of the coping suggestion for dealing with loneliness in chapter 7 might also be helpful.

EXERCISE: Emotional Needs

Take a few minutes to reflect on some of your treasured memories of intimacy with your partner. Aside from the sexual aspects of those times, were any of your emotional needs met (either fully or in part)? Then, in your journal, identify five such needs. After you've identified them, write about any ways you might be able to satisfy each need that don't involve sexual contact, are free of sexual overtones, and won't make you feel either guilty or ashamed.

SENSUAL NEEDS

Sensuality and sexuality often overlap, but they don't have the same meaning. *Sexuality* means sexual arousal, the desire for sexual union, and actual sexual contact. *Sensuality* means heightened awareness and enjoyment of our five senses. You don't need sex for your body to feel alive. Savoring each bite of an apple or swimming in shimmering waters can do that for you.

EXERCISE: Nonsexual Sensual Needs

Do you feel that having more nonsexual sensual experiences might prove helpful to you? If so, take a few minutes to recall any enjoyable nonsexual and shame-free experiences that brought you sensual pleasure. Then, start a new page in your journal entitled "Dealing with Nonsexual Sensual Needs," and answer the following question: "What have I enjoyed eating, seeing, hearing, tasting, smelling, or touching that didn't involve sex and didn't make me feel guilty?"

Some women find comfort and delight in these: perfume, scented lotions, scented candles, soft or silky clothing, exercise, sports, steam baths, sauna baths, massage, hot showers, dancing, playing or listening to music, singing, preparing tasty dishes, kneading dough, holding babies, grooming pets, and enjoying nature, art, and other forms of beauty.

Now, in your journal, list five sensual experiences that were or might be enjoyable. Don't restrict yourself to the suggestions listed above. If you become uncomfortable as you follow through with any of the suggestions on your list, stop what you are doing and try something else.

SEXUAL JEALOUSY

Jealousy is the name of the resentment we feel for someone who has something we want but do not have, whether it be a quality, position, relationship, advantage, or an aspect of an unfulfilled dream. *Jealousy* involves the fear that we may never get what we want or that we may lose what we have. *Sexual jealousy* refers to our loathing for anyone we feel or suspect is competing with us for our partner's love or who might diminish our worth to our partner.

Sexual jealousy can go both ways. Both you and your partner may fear the consequences of sexual deprivation. At the same time, each of you may have an intense empathy for one another's hardships and feel guilty about harboring such jealous fears.

Sue, who is the wife of a private, first class, in the U.S. Army, puts it this way: "Kevin's looking at other women never bothered me much before he went overseas, but when he does it now, I wonder if he cheated on me while he was gone. I trust him, but it would be only natural for him to have become so lonely or so scared that he just had to be with someone. Maybe I would do the same if I was in a war zone. My best friend asked me, 'Why are you so insecure? Kevin's a quality guy. He wouldn't do that to you. Besides, he was probably too busy staying alive over there to be thinking about sex.'

"My cousin says, 'A man's a man. How can you think that Kevin, living at death's door, could stay celibate? There's no need to be jealous, though. It's you he loves.'

"Frankly I don't know what to think. But if Kevin was unfaithful, I'd be crushed, same as he'd be, if I was untrue. Kevin assures me I'm still attractive, but every time he sneaks a peek at another woman now, I feel dowdy. It's irrational, I know, but that's how I feel, and it hurts."

Jealousy Is Normal

Even if you're as attractive as a cover girl, it's normal to seethe with envy when another woman flirts with your partner or when he seems charmed by her. Most women want to be foremost in their partner's heart. However, women in your position—women who toil on the home front while their partner works a dangerous job—often feel they've earned first place the hard way. So, when they suspect that they are no longer the primary woman in their partner's life, their feelings of resentment and hurt can be devastating. A soldier would feel the same way if his Purple Heart was ripped from his uniform and given to someone else.

It is beyond the scope of this book to address extreme cases of jealousy that require professional attention: for example, instances where jealousy disrupts personal functioning, threatens to dissolve a relationship, or arises from infidelity. The following exercises are appropriate only for low-to-moderate jealousy. They use jealousy to tap into unused potential.

Jealousy: Negative and Positive

Jealousy has both negative and positive aspects. *Negative jealousy* is based on the false idea that if your rival were weakened or no longer existed, you'd get what you want. However, getting rid of the competition would not give you the success you desire. For example, if you were jealous of a woman's tennis skills, her relocation or death clearly wouldn't improve your tennis skills. Lessons and lots of practice are required to improve your game.

In situations where *positive jealousy* exists, someone displays traits you have or could have, but haven't developed or are afraid to develop. An effective way to cope with this type of jealousy is to redirect its energy to developing your untapped talents or working toward your goals. The first step, however, is learning to be compassionate to your jealousy. Jealousy hurts. The disappointments and frustrations that created your jealousies can be extremely painful.

EXERCISE: Positive Jealousy

In this exercise you will learn to cope with jealousy by breaking it down into smaller pieces, then examining each separate jealousy to identify aspects that might be changed and those that cannot be changed. Start a new page in your journal entitled "Dealing with Jealousy," and answer the following questions:

1. Who are you jealous of and why? Begin by identifying one person and the reasons that person sparks your envy. If there are others of whom you are jealous, identify them and the reasons

for your jealousy. (If you wish, later on, you can expand this list.) Be specific. Avoid generalities like, "Pat, because she's prettier than me." Name specific attributes: "Pat, because she has curly hair, she never worries about her weight, and she has a dependable sister," and so forth.

2. Review your list of jealousies. What are the wishes and hopes that underlie each jealousy?

3. Which of these wishes or hopes are unattainable due to circumstances beyond your control? Any unfulfilled dreams you've listed must be grieved for and you're entitled to grieve for them.

4. Review your list of jealousies once more. Which of the traits, abilities, positions, or advantages you envy could you possibly acquire for yourself someday, either in whole or in part? For each entry, identify two steps you could take that would move you toward having the specific trait, ability, position, or advantage that is the source of your envy.

CHAPTER 9

Time and Money

"At my grocery store, they call me the 'Coupon Queen.' If I use coupons on sale items and I shop when they put out the day-old discounted baked goods, I can leave the store with a hundred dollars worth of groceries for less than forty dollars," explains Nicole, whose expert money management has kept her family out of debt. Every Sunday she maps out the week to come: "I list everything that needs to be done; put a number 1 next to what must be done; a number 2 next to tasks that are important but not top priority, and a number 3 next to those that can wait.

"I schedule time for the number 1's on my calendar in ink. And I keep a list of the rest of the tasks nearby. If I get to them fine; if I don't, the world won't come to an end. As I go through the week, I revise my schedule as I need to.

"Every morning I organize my time using the same method: assigning a 1, 2, or 3 to each task. At various times in the day, I might have to change my priorities again. I call it 'chaos management.' It keeps me from feeling scattered and wasting time. After years of driving myself crazy, I've learned to leave at least an hour a day for the unexpected."

Time and money management issues are concerns for most people who have to work for a living. Hopefully, the suggestions you'll find here will help to ease some of the time and money pressures that can cause unwelcome clashes between even the most loving of couples.

THE DILEMMA OF MULTIPLE ROLES

If you are working or going to school, you may have found that you are expected (or you expect yourself) to carry on with family responsibilities as if you were full-time homemaker. Juggling the roles of partner, worker/student, homemaker, and others like mother or caretaker of elderly relatives, can create conflicts. Competing demands for your time are a major problem, along with the expectation that today's woman can "do it all" (including attending to her appearance) and "do it all perfectly" without fatigue, anxiety, or complaint. A common, costly response to this expectation is the effort to be a "superwoman" to avoid guilt from within.

Role conflict and the pressure of trying to be a superwoman also afflict stay-at-home women. If you are a full-time homemaker, you may be seen as "not working." Yet every woman is a "working woman," especially mothers. Being at home involves multiple roles, like cook, launderer, and chauffeur, to name a few, and these roles often conflict.

For example, mothering one child can conflict with taking care of another child or with housecleaning. Because you are at home, you may feel (or be made to feel) that you must excel at homemaking and you must help out at volunteer activities, as if you had many servants and few cares about your partner's safety. Although you often go to bed at night exhausted, your efforts may not be considered "real" work by others.

Whether you earn a paycheck or not, your image of what a woman ought to feel, and what she ought to want, may clash with how you experience yourself and what reality demands of you. Over time, you may find yourself doing more and more. The expectations of your personal strengths may increase as your tasks increase. But the recognition of the strengths needed to do these tasks may not increase and, in some cases, may have faded. This lack of recognition can damage your self-esteem, especially if you see your problems as indicative of your inability to manage, rather than as the result of wearing so many hats.

In the midst of so many activities, you may neglect yourself. You may have postponed emotionally or spiritually fulfilling activities and even needed medical attention. You must learn to "mother yourself" as readily as you would your partner or children. If you don't practice self-nurturance, your physical and emotional reserves will become depleted, and you will be unable to continue being as strong as you are now. Self-care should be the foundation of your strength.

Too often, people who accomplish a great deal are taken for granted and are seldom congratulated as they deserve. If this is so for you, you need to learn to congratulate yourself. You also need to make time for activities you enjoy that don't involve taking care of others or your household. Many women find great solace in ceramics, music, or other activities they engage in just for their own satisfaction and pleasure.

Coping with Multiple Roles

The following exercises are designed to help you appreciate your strengths and to restructure some of your activities so they are more reflective of your whole being. Moreover, they should help you to put the brakes on making impossible demands of yourself. These exercises address the mental stress caused by the feeling that there are mismatches between what you do and your own nature, and the feeling that you aren't reaping the rewards of your efforts.

EXERCISE: Your "Shoulds" List

Think of all the "shoulds" you've learned regarding your role as a woman (in general) or as a girlfriend, wife, mother, daughter, or especially worker. Often these "shoulds" cause intense, recurring guilt feelings as you try to make your own choices. Even today, it is still hard to escape the pressures to adhere to the most stereotyped, traditionally feminine ways. Now, open a new page in your journal, and write "Shoulds" at the top of the page. Then, draw three columns below it. (Note that you may need more than one page to complete this exercise.)

1. In the first column, list as many shoulds as you can remember. Include those you heard when you were growing up, as well as those that you hear now: from your parents, partner, children, neighbors, friends, employers, and the media.

2. In the second column, list the source of the should; that is, where you learned it.

3. In the third column, describe what happened to you in the past when you did not live it up to a particular should. For example, were you scolded, rejected, or punished?

4. Review your list and then answer the following questions in your journal: (a) How did it feel to list your shoulds? (b) Which shoulds do you wish to keep? To change? To discard? (c) Do you see the shoulds as goals to be striven for, or as measures of your self-worth?

5. Write about how you feel when you do not live up to the expectations of these shoulds. What do you say to yourself? How does this compare to what other people say to you? Are you doing or saying anything that makes things worse? What makes you feel okay when you deviate from your shoulds? What makes you feel not okay when you deviate?

JUNK VERSUS JOY

Think about what is truly important about being a partner, mother, or worker. What kind of person do you want to be in relation to the people who matter to you? Which of your qualities do you really want to share with them? What activities are really necessary in each role? For example, what is it to be a mom? Is there a difference between loving and baking cupcakes? Does baking the cupcakes ever get in the way of loving?

EXERCISE: Junk Versus Joy

Now, open a new page of your journal and call it "Junk Versus Joy." Draw a line dividing the page in half. Label one side "joy," the other "junk." Underneath the labels, list the junk versus joy of your various roles. Could your life be restructured so you have more of the joy and less of the junk?

Exercise: Visualizing Yourself as a Success

If you see yourself as incapable of succeeding at something new, this exercise can help you learn to see yourself as a someone who learns new skills easily.

Relax for a few minutes, then close your eyes.

1. Visualize a particular specific aspect of your life in which you feel inadequate or incompetent. Pick a definite and concrete instance in which you have not succeeded thus far and in which you feel you may never succeed. (Take three to four minutes to do this.)

2. Now visualize yourself as succeeding at this particular task. (Take another three to four minutes.)

3. Think about the steps you would need to take to turn your success fantasy into a reality, and make a commitment to begin working to achieve this success.

THIRTEEN TIME SAVERS

1. Prioritize your activities and map out your day accordingly, thus reducing the anxiety that can be caused by indecision, or the fear of not completing essential tasks.

2. Combine activities as often as is reasonable. Relatively mindless activities (such as folding laundry, washing dishes, peeling vegetables, filing, stretching, deep-knee bends, and certain other exercises) can be combined with watching television or a movie, listening to music or a book on tape, or making phone calls that don't require your full attention.

   Caution: Do not multitask if you are negotiating financial arrangements or speaking with employers or distraught relatives or friends. It is also downright dangerous to do two things at once while taking care of children, driving, or handling dangerous substances or objects such as boiling water, hot oil, poisons, or knives. Stop combining activities as soon as you begin having memory problems, making mistakes, dropping or misplacing objects, or feeling upset or tired.

3. Some warehouses, pharmacies, and grocery stores provide free or low-cost delivery service. Order staples like canned goods, toilet paper, cleaning supplies, school supplies, and other nonperishable nonbreakable items online and have them delivered. Even with a

delivery charge, such staples still may cost less than buying them at retail prices, and you save time as well.

4. Route your errands in a time-efficient manner. Plan them so you don't have to backtrack. Find stores, doctors, and other service providers that meet your needs and that are on the way to your workplace or other places you drive to regularly.

5. "A place for everything and everything in its place" should be your motto. Without becoming a perfectionist, try to organize your home by categories: for example, keep all your financial papers in the same location; all your unpaid bills in the same spot; and so on. You decide the categories. It may take some time to improve the organization of your home, but it takes far less time to find a needed medication when all your meds are stored in the same general area rather than scattered throughout your home.

6. Let a kitchen timer, not you, keep track of the time when you have only a limited amount of time to spend on particular activity.

7. Take a break from whatever you are doing after you've made your second dumb mistake (like putting your keys in the freezer) or when you are hungry, tired, or upset. Taking time to tend to your own needs will save you the time and effort involved in correcting your errors.

8. Take care of medical problems promptly. The longer you wait, the more your problem will worsen, resulting in more visits to the doctor, greater expenses, and a longer recovery time.

9. Avoid scheduling appointments and activities during heavy traffic times; do some research for alternative routes to avoid heavy traffic; check your local paper or

radio station for information on road conditions, changes in public transportation, and other possible transportation problems.

10. Minimize waiting time for medical appointments by scheduling appointments at the beginning of the day or right after lunch. If the appointment is first come, first served, arrive early.

11. Confirm all appointments.

12. Identify your time wasters and make appropriate changes in your schedule.

13. Ask others how they save time, take a time management course, or a read a book on time management.

DISAGREEMENTS ABOUT MONEY

It's frustrating and painful, and can be downright enraging, to work hard yet still not have enough money to pay for basic necessities, much less for emergencies or some small pleasures. "How did our marriage come to this?" asked Tanya, the wife of a reservist. "Sometimes it seems that all we talk about is money, and that every decision we make about everything depends on our bank account, not on what we really want in life. Life shouldn't be all about money, but that's how it is sometimes. We shouldn't take it out on each other either, but we do.

"It's not my fault. It's not his fault. But when I have to wait until the next paycheck to visit my sick mother, I get depressed, then I explode. Usually it's over something small—well—not that small. Like him buying an expensive tool without discussing it with me first.

"I asked him Saturday, 'If we can afford that, how come I can't go to see my mom?' And he said, 'How about all that money you spend on clothes?' 'I get them at thrift stores,' I answered.

"'You're ruining my day off,' he said back. So, I told him it's my day off, too, and that he just ruined it by being so selfish. Then he called me selfish back and before anyone could say 'Cut it out,' we're yelling at each other. All this makes me so sad I want to cry."

When people live on a shoestring budget and don't see any way to improve their finances, they often begin feeling deprived and powerless. When they feel so trapped, they often take out their frustrations on someone else (or on themselves). Hence, even devoted partners may find themselves acting as if their partner was responsible for inflation and high interest rates or other economic factors that contribute to their financial miseries. Sometimes, they even put each other down for not earning more money, or for buying personal items of minor value.

Disagreements can become especially heated when they are not only about money, but also about the emotional meaning of the money. If he spends more on himself than you do, does that mean his needs or his contributions to the family are more important than yours? If you usually get your way about money, does that mean you also get your way about where to spend the holidays or other important matters? Sometimes money disputes are also about the need for more love, attention, or sex; about hurt feelings and other resentments; or about issues unrelated to money or to your relationship.

For example, Tanya and her husband realized they had more arguments about money after visits from their parents. Clearly, parental visits brought up unresolved issues from their personal past lives.

COPING WITH MONEY ISSUES

Eliminating all struggles over money is impossible. Even rich people argue about money. There are, however, ways of handling financial disagreements so they don't escalate into major disputes. Consider some of the suggestions below as well as those in appendix 1, Guidelines for Effective Communication. You can modify all suggestions to fit your specific needs. You'll need to purchase a separate notebook or journal to use as a finance journal to keep track of your work as you implement some of the suggestions below.

1. **Don't use finances as a club.** If you give up some-
    thing for your partner's sake, turn don't around and
    repeatedly complain about it or refer to it as proof that
    he is inconsiderate. The same holds true for your part-
    ner. If you feel you have been shouldering most of the
    sacrifices, you need to say so, directly not indirectly,
    for example, by mocking your partner. The same holds
    true for your partner. If he feels he is shouldering most
    of the burden, he needs to tell you that.

2. **Identify and acknowledge each partner's financial
    contributions.** You may be more aware of the ways in
    which you've failed to live up to your own financial
    expectations, or to your partner's expectations, than of
    the many ways you contribute to the economic
    well-being of your family. Also, the same may hold
    true for your partner. The following exercise will help
    both of you to recognize your many tangible contribu-
    tions:

    Open two new pages in your finance journal, one
    for you and one for your partner. Entitle each page
    "Financial Contributions to the Family," and draw
    three columns on each page. Label the first column
    "Activity"; the second, "Hours per Week"; the third,
    "Amount Earned." Both pages should be identical. In
    column 1, list all the types of work you do that benefit
    the family; in column 2, the approximate number of
    hours you spend on that activity; in column 3, the
    amount of money earned. Use one page to figure out
    your contributions, and have your partner figure out
    his contributions on the second page.

    Be sure to list not only paid work but also the
    many essential tasks you and your partner perform to
    keep your home and your family functioning properly.
    Certainly, the time you spend figuring out how to save
    money, for example, by cutting out sale coupons, scan-
    ning the newspaper or Internet for bargains, or

researching price comparisons must be considered valid work. There are many other tasks you perform for which you may get little or no credit, and which go virtually unrecognized by praise or money.

Yet couples therapists Gottman and Silver (1999) have identified at least one hundred reoccurring tasks involved in keeping a household functioning, including buying food and preparing meals; making beds, recycling; cleaning the kitchen and bathroom; doing the laundry; replacing sundries like soap and paper napkins; and taking care of the hundreds of medical and educational needs of young children. Then there are the efforts made to promote one another's careers; chauffeuring family members to work or school; taking care of the garden or pets; and dealing with household service providers.

For each of the unpaid tasks you perform, estimate the amount of time required as well as the cost of hiring someone to replace you: for example, what would it cost to have someone check the air in your tires, mow the lawn, babysit the children, pick up a family member from the airport, or host a party? Ask your local librarian or employment office to assist you in finding out the current wages for these services. At the very least, these tasks would receive minimum wage. Keep in mind that many of the tasks traditionally allocated to women, such as homemaking and child care, are considered inferior work, unimportant work, or not even work at all. Thus the market value of these labors rarely reflects their true value to the family.

Next, share your lists with each other. Add up the number of hours and financial contributions for each partner for their paid and unpaid labor. Reading your completed lists aloud to each other will help you to better appreciate each other's contributions, as well as your own.

3. **Hold business meetings.** When you talk about money issues, envision yourselves as business partners holding a meeting to decide how to best allocate the funds at their disposal. Often, several meetings are required, during which time certain steps are taken, some of which are listed below. Consider using the following steps as well, modifying them as needed.

- **Disentangle money issues from other issues.** When you're discussing money, don't stop to criticize each other's relatives or friends. Ask yourselves, "What would I be upset about if I didn't have to worry about money? What would we argue about if we had a million dollars in the bank?" Then you will have a list of problems that are not primarily about money. Agree that you will set these issues aside. If you wish, you can deal with them another time. For the moment, your focus is on money.

- **Look at the facts.** Get a truthful picture of your financial situation. Compare your total assets to your expenses; your yearly income to your yearly expenses. If your income varies from one year to the next, determine your average income for the past three to five years. Determine how much money is available now versus how much is tied up in real estate, retirement, or other long-term investments. Identify essential expenses like food, housing, basic medical care, and so forth. After paying for essentials, how much money is left?

- **If you do not have this information, make a plan to get it.** Review your income tax returns and other financial papers or keep track of your expenses for one or two months. Don't forget to keep track of incidentals, such as vending-machine snacks, cigarettes, and other small purchases that sometimes can add up to several hundred dollars a month. When you estimate your monthly or yearly expenses, take into account seasonal needs, real estate or other taxes, insurance premiums, gifts, vacations, anticipated medical or home repair expenses, car maintenance, and all other expenses that do not appear on a regular or monthly basis.

- **Compile a list of the financial issues, large or small, that confront your family.** Don't try to decide which problems are more important than others. That comes later. For each situation, estimate the amount of money involved. If you don't have enough information to make a reasonable estimate, make a plan for obtaining it.

- **Prioritize.** Rank order the issues you listed in the question above. Identify the most pressing problems and those that can wait (and for how long). If you aren't in total agreement, start with the ones that you both consider priorities. For each priority item, develop a list of possible solutions. If necessary, consult with a financial specialist or with knowledgeable friends or relatives, or conduct further research on the issue yourselves.

- **Break down larger financial problems into smaller separate parts.** They're much easier to tackle when they are separated in this way.

- **Tackle the easiest problems first.** Often these can be solved more quickly than complex issues or those problems involving large amounts of money. By clearing the decks of smaller issues, you can focus on the more difficult ones with less distraction. **Caution:** Don't stay stuck on smaller issues to avoid dealing with the larger ones.

- **Start anywhere.** If you can't decide which problem to deal with first, just pick one at random. You have to start somewhere.

- **Look for ways to compromise.** Even small compromises can promote a sense of partnership rather than conflict. However, compromise is not always possible. Special credit must be given to every family member every time he or she must do with less for the sake of all.

- **Be honest.** Before making decisions as a couple, try to be as clear as possible about what you want as individuals. Suppose you want to buy a dishwasher and your partner wants a new washer and dryer. Reaching a joint decision becomes much harder if one (or both) of you aren't really sure you want what you say you do. If you aren't certain about a particular matter, say so.

- **Make plans to discuss your finances again.** At the end of each meeting, set up a tentative time and agenda for the next meeting. If preparation will be needed, decide who will do what and by when. Be specific.

- **If you can't work this out, get help.** If you can't complete these steps because of quarreling, you may need the help of a mental health professional or another mediator.

ELEVEN WAYS TO SAVE MONEY

1. **Buy in bulk and split the cost with others.** Share costs of books, rental movies, carpet shampoo machines, and other items with friends and relatives.

2. **Use your library.** Most libraries stock CDs, audio-tapes, and videos. Some libraries lend tools and toys. They also have reference services and information on free or low-cost entertainment, and medical and other services offered in the community. (Such help also may be available in local newspapers.)

3. **Reduce credit card debt by using cash, checks, or debit cards and by paying off your balances as soon as possible.**

4. **Contact local medical and dental schools or medical research facilities to inquire about free or low-cost medical services.** Some schools offer opportunities to participate in research that provide treatments to research participants.

5. **Take an inventory of your belongings.** You might be less tempted to buy another black skirt, teapot, lamp, or toy if you know you already have three of the item at home. Before you buy anything, ask yourself, "Do I really need this? Am I positive or can I sleep on it and decide later?"

6. **Usable, presentable, almost-new clothes, house-wares, and other items can be purchased online or at thrift stores and yard sales.** Discount stores sell books, carpets, toys, furniture, clothing, appliances, and similar items at cut-rate prices. Secondhand stores located in well-to-do neighborhoods often carry luxury items and designer clothing at drastically reduced rates. **Caution:** Don't buy items you really don't need simply because they are so inexpensive compared to commercial prices.

7. **Check out consumer report ratings before making a major purchase.** Check out Better Business Bureau

listings before doing business with a contractor or company.

8. **Always check for hidden costs and possible discounts.** For all financial transactions of significance ask, "Are there any additional costs or is this the absolute final price?" Inquire about any penalties regarding return or withdrawal policies. Any terms that aren't in writing somewhere (on a receipt, Web site, or brochure) need to be put in writing, signed and dated.

9. **Check for duplicate charges, faulty totals, and other billing errors on all bills.**

10. **Don't leave receipts scattered in your purse or on the kitchen table.** As soon as you get home, file them in a waterproof file or an envelope set aside for that purpose. Or develop another system to keep track of receipts.

11. **Read a book on frugal living or money management.** See appendix 2, Resources, for selected titles.

In this chapter, you learned about some ways of managing your time and money more effectively. These methods cannot eliminate all of your time and money pressures, but they can help to lighten the many burdens such pressures impose on your already burdened life.

CHAPTER 10

Children

Although you cannot promise your children that their father will be safe forever, your ability to respond effectively to their emotional needs and to their difficult questions can make an enormous difference in their lives. This chapter deals with some of the reactions common among children who have parents employed in dangerous occupations. It offers ways for you to help your children cope with the uncertainties of their father's work.

CHILDREN'S MANY FEARS

First and foremost, children fear the injury or death of their father. They may equally fear the injury or death of their mother. These basic fears can lead to a host of additional fears that are described below.

Life Threat

Once children realize their father is at risk they can become worried about your safety, too. For children, the thought of losing one parent can be traumatic; the thought of losing both is even more devastating. Their major fear is this: If both of their parents die or are injured, then who will take care of them? Even if you escape injury, if their father has been hurt or killed, they may worry that you will become so distraught that you might go away, or, worse, that you won't want to take care of them anymore. Even if children don't state such fears aloud, you must bring their fears into the light of day to ease their anxiety and expose the falsity of their worries about you.

Worldview Threat

The nature of their father's dangerous work requires his children to encounter human error and malice. This awareness—that the world is not always safe, orderly, or just—is painful. It shatters the belief that being good, smart, or careful enough is a protection against harm, leading to a feeling of powerlessness. Like adults, children can be humiliated by such feelings.

Talk to your kids about what it means to them that life can be unfair. As difficult as this may be, consider asking them to think about questions like these: "If it's true that innocent people suffer sometimes, then what do we do? Suppose your father—who does all he can to be good at his job and good to others—is shot, but others—who are lazy or do bad things—never get hurt. Does that mean we should stop trying to be good, or decide that most people are bad?"

Emphasize to your children that terrible events are beyond their control and that, no matter how horrible those events may be, they cannot destroy your love for them or the importance of living life fully and honorably. For example, you could say, "I may not be sure about everything, but I know that bad things aren't caused by something you or I or your father did. I'm also sure that your father and I will always do our best to take care of you. And no matter what bad things might happen, it's important to care about other people, to learn new things about the wonderful world we live in, and to enjoy life."

Perhaps you have a spiritual framework or another type of worldview that can help your children make sense of life's cruelties. But if these issues confuse you, you are not alone. They have perplexed some of the greatest spiritual teachers. Rather than avoid the subject because you don't have all the answers, consider sharing some of your conflicting thoughts with your children, if that seems appropriate. Or perhaps one of these statements reflects your views: "I don't know why bad things happen. I wish I had answers for you, but I don't. What if nobody does? What if that's just the way things are?"

Discussions about the meaning of tragic events are usually appropriate for pre-teen and teenage children, not younger ones. Prior to the teen years, children tend to think in concrete, not abstract, terms. Do not initiate discussions about philosophical concepts with younger children. Limit any discussion of such issues to answering their questions and reassuring them that you love them and that they are not the cause of negative events beyond their control. See the section "Keep Your Child's Age in Mind" later in this chapter for additional suggestions.

EMOTIONAL OVERLOAD

Children have trouble separating their sense of self from their feelings. For them, feeling a strong emotion doesn't mean that the emotion is only one part of a wide spectrum of feelings, but that it constitutes their entire being. They feel as though that one emotion is all of them. For example, they may think that feeling very angry will cause them to explode. Hence, when the "bomb" of their feelings goes off inside them, they may find themselves even more afraid than the adults who live with them. For children, their feelings seem to control them, and they think and feel there is little they can do about that.

Self-Ideal Threat: Decreased Self-Esteem

Feeling threatened on so many levels can cause children to act, think, or feel in ways that contradict their view of themselves or the ways they believe others expect them to be. This difference, between their ideal image of themselves and their actual behavior, is a blow to their self-esteem. Under stress, normal children sometimes behave as if they were younger than they are. For example, five-year-olds may want baby bottles; ten-year-olds may want younger children for play-mates; and teenagers may want to be held as if they were small children. Although such behavior can provide some comfort, it also can be a cause of shame and embarrassment.

Children's Anger

When children encounter the painful truth that no one is safe from harm, they then realize that their parents cannot guarantee their safety. Even if children understand logically that their parents are only human, on some level they may feel betrayed by and angry at them. Often children's anger at their parents for not being all-powerful becomes entangled with their anger at their own powerlessness. Children may direct their anger at both parents equally; or they may feel more anger for one parent than the other; or they may become angry with others.

Anger can be expressed directly through negative behavior or indirectly through emotional withdrawal. Either way, family tensions result, creating even more insecurity in the children and more stress for the parents. Moreover, some children fear that if their parents find out how scared and angry they are, their parents will reject or abandon them. Their guilt at being angry at their parents and their confusion over that fact—at the very time they most need their parents—can result in even more problem behavior and communication difficulties.

COMMON EMOTIONAL AND BEHAVIORAL REACTIONS

As a result of their many fears, children can develop a variety of emotional and behavioral problems. Some of the most common include the following:

Pre-school age: Bed-wetting, thumb sucking, baby talk, fear of sleeping alone, stomach cramps or headaches, listlessness, and defiance.

Grade-school age: Any of the symptoms common to pre-school children listed above, and any or all of the following behaviors: sleep problems (nightmares, night terrors, insomnia, frequent awakenings, fear of sleeping in strange places, climbing into bed with parents); anxiety about the future; confusion (difficulties in making decisions or concentrating); emotional numbing; boredom; irritability, anger, and mood swings; negative self-statements ("I'm stupid/ugly/a loser/a wimp"); extreme changes in eating patterns (overeating or not eating); crying for no apparent reason; headaches and stomachaches; withdrawal from friends and family; and problems at school and with peers.

Adolescents: Any of the symptoms common to pre-school or school-age children listed above, and any and all of the following behaviors: addiction (alcohol, drug, and food abuse); sexual acting out; and excessive use of sarcasm.

Vulnerable Children

Some children are more vulnerable to developing symptoms than others: for example, disabled children and children who must cope with problems or changes at home or at school; a period of life transition, such as entering puberty; a major disappointment or medical illness; or a death or serious illness in the family. Often such children need help in separating their fears about their father's safety from their fears about another disturbing situation.

When Should You Be Concerned About Your Child's Symptoms?

Symptoms that appear after recent threats to a child's safety are to be expected. These threats could be their father's assignment to a dangerous job; news of injuries or deaths in their father's occupation; the illness or death of a family member, friend or friend's parent, or pet; money problems; or rising neighborhood crime. A single infrequent symptom that improves over time is not as much of a concern as a child with several symptoms, some of which seem to be worsening.

Nevertheless, it is highly recommended that you consult with a school counselor or with a trained mental health or medical professional if your child exhibits any of the symptoms listed above or other symptoms of concern. Furthermore, more than three symptoms; one or two weeks of the same symptom with no sign of improvement; major decline in school performance; ongoing withdrawal from others; fire setting; frequent expressions of suicidal thoughts or plans; or feelings of worthlessness or helplessness indicate that you need to seek help immediately.

HELPING CHILDREN COPE

You can help your children by building their personal strengths and making their world as physically and emotionally safe as possible. You also need to speak to them about their irrational fears, as well as their rational ones, and about any other concerns they may have. Do not be concerned that you will upset your children by doing so. Your children are already upset about these matters. Open discussions can provide relief, as well as ideas for constructive action. They are also an opportunity for you to give your children accurate information and teach them how to calm themselves. If your child is too young to put thoughts and feelings into words, nonverbal methods like drawing or acting out their feelings may be beneficial.

As you go about helping your children, be gentle with yourself. You have many obligations and you cannot expect to respond to them perfectly on every occasion. Even if you don't see immediate results or you feel you made a mistake or "could have done better," remember that children pick up the caring behind your efforts. This in itself strengthens them.

Keep Your Child's Age in Mind

You will need to adapt the suggestions in this chapter to your child's unique personality and particular need at the time. Note that an approach that works for one child may not help for another; it may be helpful in one situation, but not in another. You will also need to keep in mind your child's age. For example, don't talk to your pre-adolescent children as if they were adults, even if they are taller than you are.

Until the age of two, children understand the world primarily through their senses: that is, through touching, hearing, tasting, and seeing. They have little awareness of the various threats described in this chapter. Symptoms may develop, however, because of increased tensions in the home. For children of this age, cuddling is more effective than logical discussions.

Between the ages of two and seven, children tend to believe they are the cause of most events. When you tell them that they don't have the power to cause a parent's illness, injury, departure, or emotional stress, they may be able to repeat your words, but they may not comprehend the meaning of your words. But keep on telling them it isn't their fault. At some indefinite point of time in their development, your message will sink in because you will have firmly implanted it in your children's memory.

From about the age of seven to the teen years, children's ability to comprehend reality grows by leaps and bounds, but they still have difficulty grasping abstract concepts such as "education," "safety precautions," or "democracy." Try draw a picture in their mind. Use simple rather than complex words and concrete rather than abstract terms. For instance, instead of saying, "Your dad has had lots of safety training," describe this training in specific concrete detail: for example, "Daddy went to school for a hundred hours to learn how to be safe. Now he knows how to put bandages on himself in case no one is around to help him. Maybe he can show you how to do that sometime."

Teenagers are more capable of understanding abstract concepts than younger children. However, when under stress, they can revert to earlier, more immature ways of thinking.

Teach Your Children About Feelings

Children may not be able to put their feelings into words. They may not even know the names of some of their feelings. You can play a major role in teaching your children about the nature of feelings (such as they are neither right nor wrong, and that several can be experienced at the same time); about how feelings differ from thoughts and actions; and about some of the methods people use to control their emotions.

Be sure to talk about positive feelings, as well as those usually considered negative, and instances where positive feelings would be meaningless without the co-existence of alleged negative ones. For example, you could talk about the relationship between courage and fear as follows: "Courage doesn't mean you are never afraid; it means you keep on doing what is right even though you are afraid. If there was no fear, then how could courage be courage?" See appendix 2 for books that will be helpful in such discussions.

Teach Your Children How to Calm Themselves

Teach your children how to calm themselves using deep breathing or muscle relaxation exercises, or with other methods described in the "Coping with Anxiety" section in chapter 1 and in helpful books listed in appendix 2. Experiment with different methods until you find some that work. Practice these methods with your children not only during crises or media exposure to frightening events but at other times also, so that they become well learned, almost automatic. Emphasize that a technique that works one time may not always work; that sometimes it may be necessary to repeat a technique several times, or to use more than one technique; and that they should come to you for help when the techniques aren't helping enough.

Identify Points of Stability and Support

Counter your children's fears by reminding them about the positive and stable forces in their lives. Ask yourself, "What is true and will remain true regardless of outside events? What can my children count on regardless of any future shocks?" Ethical values, religious or spiritual beliefs, and certain cultural traditions are stable and steadfast, as is your commitment to your children. The latter truth can't be stated too often to children who need reassurance.

Identify supportive adults such as relatives, neighbors, teachers, friends, or doctors and make a list of these people to give to your children. Post it on the refrigerator or near the phone. Have your children repeat the names of these individuals several times. Perhaps these people can speak to your children about the ways in which they can be supportive. Identify other sources of support, such as nearby hospitals, fire departments, emergency shelters, emergency radio channels, or relevant Web pages, books, or pamphlets. Some children may benefit from visiting a fire department or police station or other supportive civic organization.

Create and Practice Positive Self-Talk or Affirmations

Help your children create reality-based statements that affirm their abilities and inherent worthiness or that evoke the support and strengths of others. For example, "I am learning to do more and more things every day"; "I am important"; or "My parents (and _____) love me and will do everything they can to help me." Begin by asking, "When you feel scared or sad, is there anything you can say to yourself that might help you feel less scared or sad?" Note that this is a difficult question to answer, even for adults. Your children will need your help in formulating a self-statement that truly empowers them. Use the guidelines in the section "Affirmations" in chapter 1 to find suggestions you might offer to your children. However, it's best if they can come up with their own ideas or rephrase your ideas in their own words. Write down their affirmations on paper, rehearse them out loud, or draw representations of them—whatever works. Repetition is the key.

Be Present

The importance of being present when your children need to talk cannot be overstated. However, when you simply don't have the time, hopefully, you will have at least a few minutes to ask about the general nature of their concern. While talking with your children, look directly into their eyes. Some form of physical contact appropriate for their age and personality also can be helpful, such as hugging or touching their hand or shoulder. Assure your children that you will be available as soon as you can.

If possible, set up a specific time to talk about their concerns. For example, you could say: "I absolutely do want to talk about _____ with you. It's such an important subject. But right now I need to _____. How about we talk at [indicate a specific time]? Do you think you can wait that long?" Should your children need extra assurance, you could write down the time and date of your meeting on a calendar or on a piece of paper and give it to them. Of course, if your child is experiencing a crisis or is in danger, you will need to drop everything and take appropriate action.

Don't Pressure Your Children to Talk

At times, as advised by certain mental health professionals, magazine articles, and media presentations, you may feel that it is your duty to help your children "get their feelings out." However, unless they have told you they are having certain feelings, it does little good to insist that they do so. In truth, it may harm them, due to the fact that pressuring them to talk about their feelings may create even more fear. That's because such pressure may suggest they are controlled by mysterious forces hidden deep within themselves of which they are unaware.

Invite Discussion

Instead of telling your children what they think and feel, open the door to a discussion of their inner world by talking in a general terms about the various kinds of concerns experienced by families who live under the sword of Damocles. For instance, you could refer in a general way to one of the common emotions felt by children whose fathers are at risk, by referring to something you read or heard about in the news, or from a friend or neighbor. For instance, you could say, "At last night's PTA meeting, some of the teachers explained that it's normal for children to be more scared and sad and have more bad dreams if their father is away from home working somewhere dangerous." Your children can then become aware of certain emotions by being forced to admit to themselves or to you that they have experienced some of those feelings themselves.

By referring in an indirect manner to what you think may be troubling your children, you will give them unspoken permission to have these concerns and you communicate to them that you can discuss these matters without punishing or humiliating them. For example, by sharing the following personal experience, Jane, the wife of an army corporal and the mother of two children, opened the door to a series of honest discussions with her children.

■ Jane's Story for Her Children:

"When I was a little, I had lots of fun playing with a friend of mine whose name was Mattie. Her dad was a policeman. But sometimes Mattie would just start hitting me, over nothing, and sometimes she didn't want to play with me. I guess if I knew that my dad could get hurt any day, I wouldn't feel like playing all the time either. I'd probably feel like hitting too.

"Maybe you never feel like Mattie did. But if you do, it isn't bad to feel that way, and it doesn't mean you don't love your father. It's okay to be afraid when scary things are happening, or might happen. But if we talk about how we feel, we will not be as afraid. There are many things we can do to be less afraid. So if you ever feel scared, mad, or sad, I want you to come and talk to me about it. I promise I won't get mad at you or punish you, no matter what you say."

Talking and Dreaming Don't Make It So

Some children, especially younger ones, believe or fear that talking or dreaming about a negative event means it is happening right now or can make the negative event take place in the future. Assure them otherwise. Should the negative event actually be happening in the moment or eventually come to pass, their dreams, speech, or thoughts are not the cause, and they need to know that.

Let Your Children Speak First

Before you begin giving your children information and advice, ask them how they are feeling and what they know about the situation of concern. If current events have spurred their fears, what do they know about these events? Some good questions to ask are "What scares you the most?" or "What did they say on the news?" Be sure your children know the meaning of the terms they are hearing or using. They may have a limited or inaccurate understanding of terms like bombing, sniper attacks, guerilla warfare, or rioting. Or they may believe that Baghdad is two hours away by car, or that all criminals are fiendishly smart. Find out what your children know about their father's job. Their knowledge of what he does may be unclear, incomplete, or distorted.

Also, as much as you might want to provide your children with accurate information, at times it will be difficult to do that.

Authorities may disagree or there may be public debate about certain issues. However, some of your children's beliefs about their father's job and current and future events may be totally unrelated to reality.

Don't Shame Your Children for Their Fears, Support Them

In our culture, unhappy people who don't think positively most of the time are often seen as abnormal or inferior. As a result, your children may already feel ashamed of being afraid, anxious, or unhappy. Perhaps they have also been shamed by others. This makes it even more important that you assure them that having certain thoughts or feelings doesn't mean that anything is wrong with them. Emphasize that they are responsible for their behavior, not their thoughts and feelings. Also emphasize that if they talk about some of the thoughts and feelings they are ashamed of, they might be able to change or even eliminate those thoughts and feelings entirely.

Here are some examples of shaming messages:

"You're too old to be scared of _____." "Where's your head? It's ridiculous to think _____. Everybody knows that's not true." "I can't be bothered with your silly questions." "If you want to grow up to be a man, you shouldn't ask for Mommy to hold you or for a bed-time story." "Only babies _____." "Why are you asking me the same questions you asked me yesterday?"

Don't compare your child to others or to yourself: for example, "How come your sister/brother isn't as scared as you? How come you can't be brave like _____?" and "You say you want to be a _____ when you grow up. How can you expect to do that if you are so whiny, clingy, yellow, stupid as to believe _____ or be afraid of _____?"

Observe Your Child's Reactions

A little upset is to be expected. However, if a child shows extreme signs of anxiety, like shortness of breath, sweating, dizziness, or any of the symptoms listed in the Cautions section in the introduction, stop discussing fearful topics and try to calm the child.

Comfort Your Child

Physical soothing is important: hold, stroke, hug, or touch your child lightly on the hand or shoulder. Younger children can be held or gently massaged; some enjoy having their hair brushed or being bathed. Choose ways to soothe that are comfortable for everyone. Make sure your children aren't hungry, thirsty, sleep-deprived, ill, or physically uncomfortable because of room temperature or inappropriate clothing. Warm milk with honey and other traditionally soothing drinks can be helpful. Younger children may want a light on at night and access to comforting toys, cherished blankets, or other items. Keeping to a schedule and daily routine is also helpful.

Use Rituals

Through the centuries, rituals have been a source of comfort and strength. You may have rituals from your religious, cultural, or family traditions that may be helpful, and you can also create your own, such as singing a certain song, reading a comforting story, or lighting a candle.

Correct All-or-Nothing Thinking

Because so much is at stake during life-and-death events, people and situations tend to be viewed in all-or-nothing terms, that is, as being all one way or all another way. Someone is either for you or against you: there is no in-between. Whether the mission is to save lives or fight enemy soldiers, local criminals, or raging fires, extreme measures, not moderate ones, and a focus on the present are usually required. All that matters is what one is doing now, in the present, not what one did in the past or will do in the future.

All-or-nothing thinking and thinking that focuses on the present to the exclusion of the past or the future often make sense in dangerous situations. However, they may not be useful or accurate ways to think in less dangerous situations where they may create unnecessary panic and feelings of helplessness. Among children, all-or-nothing thinking can lead to ideas like "If I'm scared (sad, doing poorly at school) right now, I'll be this way forever." The truth, however, will most likely be somewhere in between. Tell your children they probably will feel afraid again. However, this doesn't mean that they'll be afraid every minute for the rest of their lives, or that they will always be as afraid as they are in the present moment. Sometimes they might feel more afraid; sometimes less. Assure them that as they grow older and learn more about how to manage fear, they probably won't be as afraid of being afraid as they are now.

There are two other all-or-nothing thoughts common among children. They are "If Dad gets hurt, our family will end"; and "Either we'll get rid of the terrorists (criminals, drunk drivers, fire setters) entirely, or they will take over." Assure your children that should their father perish, the family will never be the same, but that doesn't mean it will fall apart; that even though violent people and forces have power, their father and his coworkers have power too; that even if certain enemies cause damage, the damage may not be total or permanent.

Being hopeful is important, but don't give children an all-or-nothing message like "All is well" or " Nothing bad will ever happen," when the news media, peers, and overheard discussions present very different messages. It's also okay to tell your children you don't know what might happen. If they are old enough, you might want to explain to them some of the ambiguities and uncertainties about the situation of concern.

Separate Safety Fears from Other Fears

Help your children separate their fears for their father's safety from their fears about other matters. If your children have trouble putting their fears into words, ask them to describe the perfect life or what they wish would happen (or not happen) that would make them happy. Their responses can reveal some of their fears and suggest future courses of action.

Set Limits on Exposure to the Media

Use your judgment in determining how much media coverage of frightening events, especially reports related to their father's occupation, is helpful. Watch media presentations with your children and then discuss their understanding of what they heard. Some children have an inadequate or inaccurate understanding of what is presented on the news or elsewhere. Correct their distortions and help them process their feelings about what they have seen and heard.

Increase Your Children's Sense of Mastery

Support your children's talents and interests and encourage them to become good at something. Self-defense classes, team sports, special interest clubs, and any form of helping others can help focus their emotional energy onto something positive. Be sure your children receive regular medical checkups and that any medical or mental health problems are treated. If they are having academic difficulties, find out what resources are available and use them.

Make Your Children's World as Physically Safe as Possible

If you have not completed "Exercise: Improve the Safety of Your Living and Work Environments" and "Exercise: Your Physical Health" in terms of your children's health, in chapter 4, do so now. Make your children aware of the safety features in your home and other family property and of any safety improvements in progress, as is age-appropriate. Show them the location of smoke detectors and other safety items and teach them how to monitor or use those that they can handle safely. Ask them what might make them feel safer. If an additional bolt on the door brings relief to one of your children, there is no harm in buying and installing such an item. Do whatever you can to make your children feel safe.

CHAPTER 11

Homecoming: Readjustment Issues

He's coming home! Could any words be sweeter? When he walks through the door, your joy may know no bounds. Yet soon afterward you may be surprised—and dismayed—to find yourself feeling apprehensive, irritable, and even sad. You may wonder, "What's wrong with me? I'm not supposed to feel like this." Your partner may also be troubled by erratic emotions, sometimes feeling closer to you than ever before; other times, miles apart.

Mixed feelings are a normal part of the readjustment process. Just as adjusting to being apart was difficult, adjusting to being together again also can be stressful. This chapter describes some of the tensions typical of the readjustment period, such as emotional distancing and shifts in the balance of power, and it provides suggestions for coping. You and your partner may not experience all of the problems described here. But even if you do, this doesn't mean you don't care about each other. All families go through upheavals of some sort at this time.

Despite its inevitable tensions, the readjustment period also can be a time of great harmony and joy. Everyone may be so grateful to be together again that all problems seem to be forgotten. Homecoming presents a wonderful opportunity to iron out any existing conflicts and to reinforce or establish traditions that will further unify and strengthen your family.

MIXED FEELINGS

While apart, you and your partner learned how to manage without each other. You also had vastly different experiences. Therefore, upon reunion you may not feel as close as you were when you were more dependent on one another and spent more time together. In addition, while apart, you both were free of the day-to-day demands of an intimate relationship and were able to act without having to consider your partner's needs. For example, you may have enjoyed not needing to cook every day; he, not needing to take out the trash. Now that you are together again, you may miss the breathing room you had while apart. You may have changed in other ways as well. Even if you like some of the changes in each other, it may take a while to get used to them.

As a result of your partner's experiences, his views about himself and life in general may have changed dramatically. He has shared life-and-death experiences with certain coworkers, forging an intense bond with them that excludes you and anyone else without firsthand knowledge of his work. You may be glad he had supportive coworkers, yet still feel left out of their comradery. Also, you may have changed. Simply surviving the hardships of waiting may have boosted your self-confidence. He may be pleased that you found positive ways to take care of yourself in his absence. Yet he may also wonder whether he's less important to you now.

Unrealistic Expectations

While you were apart, you both may have forgotten each other's annoying habits and focused only on each other's positive traits. The agony of missing your partner, coupled with the fear of never seeing each other again, may have been so great that you may have thought once you were together again, all your problems would be over (or at least not bother you as much). At first, being together again may have felt like a second honeymoon. But, eventually, you were both faced with some of the same problems you had before. Only now, these problems may loom larger because they are combined with the problems resulting from the transition itself.

Coming home may have been all he wished for while he was gone, yet it also means a loss of power and adventure (Mason 1990). While away, he used weapons and expensive lifesaving or firefighting equipment, and he tried to master criminals, enemy soldiers, raging fires, floods, or even death itself. Now, with no dragons to slay, instead of making life and death decisions, he waits in long lines. After being on alert at all times, it may be hard for him to relax; after working around the clock, it may be impossible to sleep at night and to adjust to a humdrum, daily routine. He must make massive adjustments and they can affect every aspect of his being.

The thought of being held by you may have given him the courage to get through his worst moments. Yet once back in your arms, he may feel guilty about coming home alive when others did not. Or he may worry that because he isn't there, someone may be dying. He may not share these thoughts with you. He might not be fully aware of them because they are so painful. He may want to protect you. He may think, "Bad enough I had to see what I did. She doesn't need it."

Yet not sharing creates some distance between you—as if he had some of the most significant experiences in his life on another planet, one that you don't even know exists or you know about only in theory. Like him, you may not want to talk about your worst moments. Perhaps you won't want to burden him. Yet this can only add to the emotional distance between you.

EMOTIONAL DISTANCING

Being emotionally distant from one another may be fleeting or it may persist for several weeks. Even if these feelings last only a few minutes, they are painful. It hurts to feel alienated from the one you love, especially if you had longed for his homecoming as a time of overflowing affection for each other. Since feeling alienated usually coexists with a strong need to feel close, not only are these feelings painful, they also may give rise to guilt, self-doubt, and confusion.

Yet this distancing may have little to do with your true feelings for each other. Some of his emotional distance, for example, may be a carryover from his recent ordeals. As discussed in chapter 1, emotional numbing often develops during life-and-death situations. Also it can develop in situations of ongoing stress, even when there is no immediate threat to life. Thus, some of your emotional numbing may be due to the stress of waiting for his return. Upon his return, the numbing may persist because emotions cannot be turned on and off like water faucets.

HOMECOMING AND CHILDREN

If your partner's emotional distancing extends to the children, they will probably feel rejected. He may not be rejecting them at all, yet they may begin thinking they are unwanted because they aren't good enough for their father. They may think that, because why else would he be so distant from them? If they then begin to withdraw or create disturbances, they may become even less approachable or less responsive to their father when he does demonstrate his love for them. Their negative attitude may wound him, especially if he dreamed about coming home to idyllic father-child relationships.

As a result, he may pay less attention to them or he may begin to scold them over minor matters or be irritable and impatient with them in other ways. In turn, the children may become more withdrawn or unruly. The situation could escalate until everyone feels hurt but no one can talk about it. Any negative behaviors that arise may be indirect ways to express the hurt, yet they also can be ways to connect. Bickering, although unpleasant, is a way to get a response from the other person, and may even be preferable to indifference or to feeling unimportant and unloved.

Your partner may be an extremely capable and involved father. But if he hasn't recuperated from his recent ordeal, his ability to deal with the stress of parenting may be temporarily limited. Moreover, his children may spark terrible memories of suffering children he met on the job, or grief for the children of coworkers who were left fatherless. Regardless of the reasons, a vicious cycle can start up when emotional distancing on the part of one family member perpetuates emotional distancing and irritability in another member of the family.

SHIFTS IN PATTERNS OF AFFECTION

Shifts in patterns of affection contribute to this vicious cycle. Suppose that in his absence one or more of the children drew closer to you, for example, a daddy's girl became a mommy's girl. On his return, he may feel the change. If the opposite occurred, and during his absence the children made you the target of their frustrations and they continue to do so when he returns, he may be upset by this. Instead of enjoying happy times with his children that he had imagined while gone, he must chastise them for their misbehavior. Or maybe you hoped that he would lovingly end their naughtiness, but he didn't, creating further tensions between the two of you.

There may be arguments over discipline or decisions that were made about the children in his absence. That is, suppose that even though money was tight, you couldn't refuse your son when he asked, "Can't I get a cat? Daddy is gone and I don't have a Daddy anymore. Can't I at least have a cat?" Daddy may think you should have saved the money, or gotten a dog, instead.

Perhaps while he was gone, you enrolled your children in more after-school activities. But suppose they became very attached to a male activity leader or family friend during his absence; misunderstandings might develop. For example, suppose a child seems more enthusiastic about spending time with a man who helped out during your partner's absence than with him, the child's real father. In such a situation, everyone may feel guilty and angry, including you.

Also, problems may arise if in your partner's absence, you tried to comfort the children by spending extra time with them. On his return, if you discontinue these activities, your children may have grown so accustomed to them, that when you pull back, they become demanding or dejected. In these ways, it may feel as if your children are competing with your partner for your attention. If they fear that his return means you have less time and love for them, they may not warm up to him as quickly as he expects. He may feel disappointed. They may feel guilty and confused: how can they be so happy to have him back yet also be wishing to have you all to themselves again? Their inner turmoil may present still another obstacle in their interactions with him.

Other forms of competition for love and attention are also normal. Children may demand so much of their father's time that you feel shortchanged, or siblings may compete with each other for his attention. These and other shifts in the family's patterns of affection become even more complicated and volatile if there are stepchildren or half siblings in the family.

SHIFTS IN THE BALANCE OF POWER

During your partner's absence, you were in charge and the balance of power in the home shifted toward you. You may have made important decisions on your own, instead of as one of a couple. Perhaps they couldn't be postponed until his return or perhaps you couldn't contact him or didn't want to burden him. When he returns, he may feel proud that you were so resourceful in taking care of matters in his absence. But he also may resent certain decisions you made without his input or consent, especially if he believes that in doing so, you preempted his power and position in the family as the head of the household.

Now that he's back, how will he fit into the new order of things? Will he want to exert his former authority in the home, or will he gladly let you continue making decisions in family matters? Do you want a larger role, or are you anxious for him to assume some of the duties that were shifted onto your shoulders in his absence? Initially, there may be some confusion about who is responsible for what and who has the final say in important matters. If one or both of you aren't clear on what you would like, the situation may become even more confusing.

Even if you both wish to resume the same structure you had before his departure, these adaptations can't always be made quickly or without error. For example, suppose you agree that now that he's back, all decisions about money and family visits will be made jointly. However, you may be so used to handling these matters on your own that you make a major purchase or agree to visit your parents without consulting him first—as if you were on automatic pilot.

Like you, your partner may have been on automatic pilot on some issues. This can lead to predictable clashes. For example, in dangerous occupations there is an emphasis on neatness. In the military, for instance, the requirements of keeping one's living area spotless and one's weapons clean are based on the need for soldiers to be constantly ready for any contingency. Soldiers learn to equate neatness with their dedication to their country. But how do they react when they come home to messy children or a partner who is less than perfect in her housekeeping?

John, a marine, found his family's messiness intolerable. The family, in turn, found his meticulous neatness equally intolerable. He couldn't feel safe in the midst of clutter and his family couldn't relax feeling they had to constantly pick up after themselves or face his displeasure. It is important to understand that in this type of situation, no one is right and no one is wrong. The same tension between the modes of operation necessary for dangerous occupations and those necessary for family life can exist for other issues, like promptness or obeying orders quickly without question. In dangerous occupations, showing up late or taking one's time to follow an order can cost lives, including one's own. For example, suppose a police officer, firefighter, or emergency worker coming home after a long emergency call asks his son to take out the trash. The son agrees, but calls a friend first. Conflict can easily follow.

SEXUAL INTIMACY

Sex may be better than ever; however, the readjustment period also can present some of the same sexual problems discussed in chapter 8. As much as you may have been looking forward to resuming this part of your relationship, it may take some time for your bodies to return to their previous level of responsiveness to one another.

DISABILITY AND INJURY

A full discussion about severe injury is missing from this chapter. Space limitations do not permit exploration of this important issue and its enormous impact on the entire family. Even under the best of circumstances including adequate financial coverage, superb medical care, and adequate home-care services, severe injury and disability can be a nightmare for everyone. Even relatively minor injuries can be the beginning of a long complicated journey of medical procedures and time-consuming expensive home care.

It is a gross disservice to those who have sacrificed their physical well-being for the public good to praise their ability to make the best of the situation without also acknowledging their often long-term physical and emotional suffering, and the immense losses incurred by all who love them. Information on disability benefits and services can be obtained from physicians, medical insurance representatives, personnel or benefits officers; your local, county, and state social service and disability offices; disability or injury lawyers; and the National Organization on Disability (www.nod.org); the National Federation of the Blind (www.nfb.org), the National Amputation Foundation (www.nationalamputation.org) and similar organizations. Consult your local telephone directory or library for contact information on these and similar organizations. There are also many books on disability and the family. Ask your local librarian for assistance.

COPING WITH READJUSTMENT ISSUES

Coping effectively with readjustment problems is hard enough without the added burden of feeling ashamed, guilty, or angry about having them in the first place. Note that without an attitude of acceptance, the suggestions listed below will lose much of their power.

Coping Suggestions

I. **Don't panic at every problem or strong emotion.** One of the most troubling aspects of all transition periods is experiencing bouts of strong and often mixed emotions. (Even numbing is a type of emotional experience.) When these emotions (even numbing) stop you in your tracks, you might begin to panic, wondering when and if you'll ever return to "normal."

A military wife explains: "After every homecoming I felt like I was surfing on waves of emotions I didn't always understand. Fighting them was useless. I just rode with them, wondering when things were going to settle down, and when they finally did, how our life would be different than it had been. Sometimes, we made matters worse by overreacting to every bump in the road. But other times we were too slow to react and we ignored signs of real trouble."

Only time will tell which problems are serious and which are not. Some problems may even disappear. Most likely your emotional reactivity will also lessen. As you work out the snags of readjusting to one another, you can expect fewer highs and lows. However, if your inner turmoil continues, or you or another family member develop any of the symptoms listed in the Cautions section in the introduction or in the section "Common Emotional and Behavioral

Reactions" in chapter 10, follow the recommendations provided.

2. **Plan ahead.** It is always better to anticipate possible problems and discuss how you might deal with them before they occur rather than afterward. Discussions about how daily routines, decision making, and other family patterns might change as a result of his depar-ture (and change again upon his return) and how these situations might be handled are highly recom-mended. If you didn't discuss these matters before he left, do so soon after his return. Also work together to create a plan for handling predictably difficult times such as financial crunches; family visits; and anniver-sary dates of the death or injury of a coworker, family member, or friend. Some of the problems you expect may not, in fact, emerge precisely because you talked about them in advance.

3. **Follow the "Guidelines for Effective Communication."** Use the guidelines in appendix 1, Guidelines for Effec-tive Communication, and the section "Coping with Money Issues" in chapter 9 to help your discussions stay focused and to prevent them from becoming blaming sessions where each of you is put on trial and found guilty.

4. **Let others know when it's not their fault.** During the readjustment period every relationship in the family is changing, which can make every family member more sensitive than usual to any signs of rejection or disap-proval. With emotions at such a high pitch, it's easy for any family member's irritability, anger, numbness, or sadness to be taken personally by others. For exam-ple, if your partner sees you frowning, he may assume you're upset with him even if you aren't; if he doesn't want to cuddle with you, you may assume he doesn't find you desirable even when he does. The hurt

feelings that usually result from misreading one another's moods or actions as personal rejections or criticisms easily can lead to unnecessary quarrels, stony silences, or feelings of alienation.

Some of these needless conflicts can be avoided simply by letting the other people know when your bad mood or unavailability isn't their fault. If someone has indeed offended or disappointed you, but his or her behavior is not the main reason for the way you feel, this also needs to be stated. If you usually try to hide your negative feelings from others, you may think you don't need to make these kinds of announcements. Nevertheless, your true feelings may reveal themselves in your posture, facial expression, tone of voice, or some other subtle way. People who live together are amazingly astute at picking up on each other's feelings no matter how artful the disguise.

Letting others know when they aren't to blame does not mean apologizing for yourself or giving long complicated explanations about why you're feeling or acting a certain way. All that's needed are a few sentences like these: "You matter a lot to me. I'm concerned that I might be acting as if I'm criticizing or rejecting you (or am annoyed, angry, or impatient with you). But I'm not. The way I'm feeling right now is not about you. You haven't said or done or anything wrong."

You don't need to make these announcements all the time lest they become so ordinary that they aren't even heard. Be selective, but do not ignore a sigh, a downcast look, or other signs that your mood or behavior has been misinterpreted as some kind of rejection. Because children tend to think they cause most of the events in their lives, it's especially important to help prevent them from jumping to such conclusions. Use concrete examples, preferably drawn from their own lives, to help them better understand.

For example, ask them to recall a time they when they didn't want to talk or play with anyone, even their best friend. Or remind them of a time when they couldn't do something they wanted to do; couldn't have something they wanted; or were looking forward to an event and plans were canceled. You could remind them of a time when a pet or relative died or a friend moved away or a time when they were ill.

After they identify such a time, ask questions like, "Was it your friend's fault you were in a bad mood and didn't feel like talking or playing?" and "After that happened and you didn't want to talk to or be with your friend, did that mean you didn't like your friend anymore or wanted your friend to go away?" Then you can draw parallels between the situation they remember and the one they are experiencing now, stressing that a parent's temporary bad mood or unavailability isn't necessarily their fault and doesn't mean the parent thinks poorly of them.

5.   **Use reality checks.** Reality checks involve asking others if they are thinking or feeling what you think they're thinking or feeling. For example, suppose your partner is late and you conclude that he's late because he's upset with you over a particular matter. You may be right, but the only facts you have are his tardiness and your reactions to it. Reality checks such as the following might help clarify matters: "Maybe I'm off base, but I'm wondering if you're sore at me about _____? I'm not trying to start a long discussion about one of our issues. All I want to know is if I'm reading you right or not"; or say, "I need to check something out. Are you upset with me about something?"

Reality checks do not obligate either of you to discuss the issue at hand. If you would like to talk about the issue at some mutually agreed upon time in the future, you can certainly say so. However, you need to make it clear that your sole purpose is to determine whether your interpretation of his behavior is accurate. Do not imply or, worse, insist that he discuss a possibly sensitive topic right then and there. This could create friction and make reality checks unwelcome. Reality checks, like any other communication skill, should not be overused.

6. **Find nonthreatening ways to handle missteps.** Because of the inherent stresses in this period of transition, you and your partner may make a few foolish mistakes. There also may be times you handle situations as you did while living apart, rather than according to any understandings you may have reached since his homecoming. These missteps need to be accepted for what they are, missteps, not personal attacks or signs of a character flaw.

Accepting missteps doesn't mean ignoring them. Although it is not advisable to call each other on every misstep, it may be useful to point out those missteps that occur repeatedly. A friendly reminder that you've agreed to do things differently now that you are together again may be not only necessary, but welcome. Such reminders need to be previously agreed on and worded in nonthreatening ways.

If you and your partner agree that you will remind him when he starts acting like a commanding officer, your first impulse might be to say, "There you go ordering me around again. Stop treating me like a child!" Here's a more loving alternative: "I love hearing your opinion on this [name the subject] again, even though you make it sound like there's an emergency when there isn't." By the same token, you would probably feel offended if he pointed out your failure to coordinate with him by saying, "You say I'm acting like a general, but you look at you. Ha! You're twice as bad as I am." Here's a more loving alternative: "Look at me. I'm home and glad to be together with you again. How about next time you consult with me before you make a decision like that?"

Some behaviors that currently cause tensions may have served a useful purpose originally. For example, most likely being prompt and giving firm orders were essential parts of his recent work experience, just as acting independently was a requirement while you were managing on your own. Reminders that acknowledge any positive features of the problem behavior can be especially effective. Here are some examples: "I bet some of your orders saved a lot of lives." "It's amazing how disciplined you have to be in your kind of work. It takes a lot of dedication." "This family is so lucky to have someone who knows how to get things done."

Although you can suggest reminders, he needs to make the final decision about how he wants to be approached. The same holds true for you. However, sometimes even the most carefully chosen words can trigger the other person's defensiveness or retaliatory anger. Using a nonverbal way of communicating, such as a certain hand signal, may be a better idea.

7. **Strengthen family ties.** The following activities are designed to help strengthen family ties:

    ■   **Use circles.** Circles symbolize unity and encourage participation. Whenever possible and appropriate, sit in circles during family activities such as opening gifts, having discussions, or playing games.

    ■   **Regularly scheduled family activities.** Set aside a regular time for a family activity. Include backup dates in your planning in case of illness or schedule changes. Family activities don't have to be time-consuming or expensive. They can be as simple as taking a walk or watching a television program together.

    ■   **Regularly scheduled family sharing.** At dinner or on holidays, during family vacations, or at other times when the family is gathered together, sit in a circle or around a table and have everyone say one positive thing about everyone else; make a wish; tell a joke; tell about something funny or important that happened to them recently; share an interesting fact; or describe how they handled a difficult problem. If time is short, sharing can be limited to a designated number of minutes. If time is not an issue, your family members can take as long as they wish. It is important, however, for someone to keep track of the time to ensure everyone has a turn; that everyone pays close attention to the person who is sharing; and that no one uses this time to criticize or mock anyone else.

- **A family medals exercise.** In this activity, family members make medals for each other. First, give each person a piece of paper with "A Medal for _____" written at the top. Next, each person fills in the blank with the name of the family member sitting on their right. Then, each person writes two or three sentences about the reasons this family member deserves this medal. When all the explanations for the medals are finished, everyone reads what they've written out loud to the entire family and then gives the medal to the family member for whom it was intended. Young children can be helped by others.

  You can repeat this exercise using different pairs of family members or until everyone in the family has made and received a medal from everyone else. The medals could be saved in a scrapbook or displayed in a prominent place.

8. **Maintain your support system.** Upon your partner's return, in order to make time for him, you may feel you need to withdraw from the support system and the

activities you developed to help you cope with his absence. Although you may need to cut down on some of these involvements, it's important not to sever these all of these ties entirely. You can always benefit from the support of others and from activities that strengthen and nourish you. Be selective about the activities and relationships you wish to keep active. Perhaps you can stay involved in certain activities by participating in them less frequently or for shorter periods of time.

Living under the sword of Damocles means living with fear, multiple physical and emotional demands, and work-related separations and reunions. In this book you've learned some ways of managing these and other hardships so that they do not dominate your life or create unnecessary stress for you and your family.

As I have repeatedly stressed, each woman, man, and child is unique. Do not limit yourself to the suggestions in this book. Continue to learn more by reading and talking with trusted or knowledgeable others. Most of all, trust that you have the capacity to find loving, creative ways, well-suited to your particular needs and situation, to manage the many stresses in your life. Remember, too, that you and your family will be helped, not hurt, by realizing that life entails uncertainty, emotional pain, and change.

APPENDIX I

Guidelines for Effective Communication

The following suggestions are designed to help you and your partner communicate clearly and respectfully, so that talking about your problems doesn't create more frustration or hurt. However, the guidelines presented here, especially those on talking about stressful events, may only begin to address the many challenges involved in effective communication. Individual or couples counseling may also be needed. (See appendix 2, Resources, for helpful books.)

1. **Don't wait until a crisis to communicate.** Nip problems in the bud by setting aside time to talk at the first sign of a problem and by checking in with each other regularly.

2. **Find an appropriate time and place to talk.** Don't try to solve a problem when one of you is hungry, tired, or

distracted. Find a private place that is relatively free of distractions.

3. **Set time limits on your discussion.**

4. **Don't blame most of your problems on each other's work or interests.**

5. **Don't ridicule each other or each other's friends or family members.**

6. **Separate the past from the present.** Don't blast each other with feelings that belong to someone else or to some other situation.

7. **Sort out which problems belong to you; which, to him; and which, to forces beyond your or his control.** Before you share your negative reactions to something he did or said, own up to your contribution to the problem and point out the role of outside factors.

8. **Be clear about the kinds of changes you want in your relationship, and what you're willing and not willing to do to help effect these changes.**

9. **Establish ground rules.** Agree that certain behaviors are unacceptable, such as name-calling, threats, shouting, or physical violence, including self-injury, throwing things, or breaking objects.

10. **Think about what brings you together.** Before you begin your discussion, talk about what attracted you to each other in the first place, and what keeps you together today.

11. **Draw upon past successes.** Talk about how you coped as a couple when you faced problems in the past. What worked and what didn't? Can any of the

ways that proved successful in the past help you with the problems you face today?

12. **Practice active listening and paraphrase.** Before you respond to something that he has said, paraphrase what you heard and ask him if you heard him correctly. He should do the same for you.

13. **Empathize, don't moralize.** Even if you don't like what he is feeling, don't tell him he "should" have reacted differently; try to put yourself in his position. If he's just experienced a particularly stressful event, don't tell him to "stop thinking about it," "let go," "get over it," or "get a life." Never call him a "crybaby," a "whiner," or a "sissy." Similarly, he should refrain from calling you abusive names.

14. **Use "I" statements.** An "I" message is a statement about how you feel or think, about what you want or need, or about what you will or will not do. In contrast, a "you" message blames another person or situation for how you feel.

    For example, "You're driving dangerously," is a "you" message; "I'm frightened when you drive this fast. If you don't slow down, I will need to find another way home," is an "I" message. Even though you may feel the other person is wrong and that your anger at that person is completely justified, it's important to focus on what you want or need. If there is danger, however, your first priority is to protect yourself and make yourself safe.

15. **Use time-outs.** When someone's temper begins to flare, it's time to take a break.

16. **Don't take anger at face value.** As human beings, we are wired to view anger coming at us as a sign of danger, or at least as an attack on our worth. However,

anger also can be a mask for other feelings, such as sadness or confusion. It can also reflect a problem with depression, addiction, diabetes, or any number of other medical or psychological problems.

17. **Stay focused.** Although many of your problems are probably interrelated, you will get nowhere jumping from one to the other. Focus on one issue at a time.

18. **Know that some problems have no solution.** Decide which problems are solvable and which are not and work only with the solvable ones.

19. **Build the positives.** What experiences usually bring the two of you closer together? Are you willing or able to set aside time for more of such experiences? Pull out your calendars and get started.

20. **Monitor yourselves.** If one of you develops any of the symptoms listed in the Cautions section in the introduction to this book, stop your discussion and follow the directions provided there.

Talking about problems, even if you can't resolve them, helps to clear the air. Trust that, if you speak your truth in a way that respects you, while also respecting him, the tensions between you will lessen. It will then be easier to find creative ways of living together with greater harmony.

TALKING ABOUT STRESSFUL EVENTS

Not sharing difficult experiences or pretending that past sufferings have been forgotten can lead to feelings of alienation between you and your partner. On other hand, if you speak freely with each other, he may overwhelm you with accounts of horrific events and you may overwhelm him with accounts of your emotional agony. When he wasn't sharing, you may have felt excluded and shut out, but now that he is, you may feel drained, frightened, or sad. He may have similar reactions after learning about your pain.

Because there seem to be as many pitfalls to sharing on a deep level as there are to acting as if stressful events don't matter that much anyway, you may not know what's best: to talk about stressful events or to remain silent. There are no clear-cut answers. Furthermore, there is no way to share "perfectly"; that is, just enough to better understand each other but not so much as to cause undue distress or open the door to certain misunderstandings. The following suggestions, however, can help to minimize the possibility of a negative outcome.

1. **Don't push him to talk.** When he doesn't want to talk about his traumas, don't assume that he is rejecting you. He simply may not want to relive experiences he would rather forget. Someday, he may need to tell someone about all the awful things that he experienced, but it is not your role to be his healer or therapist. You can support him without assuming that responsibility, for which you are not trained.

2. **Don't push yourself to talk or listen.** There may be times you don't want to hear about your partner's traumatic experiences. This is normal and it doesn't mean you don't want to support him. There may also be times you don't want to talk about your difficult moments. This is also normal and doesn't mean you don't want to be close to him. Like him, you are entitled to your limits. There is no rule that people who love each other must tell each other everything.

3. **Avoid extremes.** In general, extremes, such as saying practically nothing about one's struggles or true feelings, or the opposite, sharing every detail and every feeling, are to be avoided. Also, try not to share everything at once, but in little bits, with breaks in between, so you have time to digest what you've heard

or shared and to recuperate from any strong emotions you may have experienced.

4. **Let your "gut feelings" be your guide.** If you feel you've said enough or heard enough, say so, but in a gentle caring manner. Encourage him to do the same. If you aren't sure about whether or not to share a personal matter with him or hear about one of his traumatic experiences, wait until you are sure. At the very least, give yourself a few days to mull it over. It's possible you may decide to share some, but not all, aspects of your personal pain or to listen to some, but not all, of his experiences.

5. **Ask each other how to be supportive.** If he does open up to you, you may wonder what to say or if you should say anything at all. Ask him how you can best support him. If he doesn't know, you can figure it out together as you go along. Similarly, he can ask you how best to support you should you choose to tell him about some of your most trying moments. When you feel "stuck" about how to support each other, the best question to ask may be "Is there anything I can do to help?"

Resources: Organizations and Suggested Readings

The organizations and materials listed here are by no means all of the resources available. You are encouraged to seek additional help by spending some time on the Internet or at your local library, or by talking to helping professionals.

ADDICTIONS: ALCOHOL AND DRUG ABUSE/EATING DISORDERS

Organizations

Names of treatment centers specific to a particular addiction or eating disorder can be obtained from the phone book, hospitals, city or county mental health or social service agencies, your or your partner's employee and family support programs, or 12-step programs such as Alcoholics Anonymous (www.alcoholics-anonymous.org); Narcotics

Anonymous (www.na.org); Overeater's Anonymous (www.overeaters anonymous.org); Al-Anon and Ala-Teen (www.al-anon-alateen.org); Adult Children of Alcoholics (www.adultchildren.org); and Nar-Anon (http://alcoholism.about.com/od/naranonresources/). Information about 12-step programs can also be obtained from your telephone directory or local library.

Books and Other Recommended Materials

Books and other materials on various forms of addiction are available through the 12-step programs listed above and through Hazelden Educational Materials, Box 176, 15251 Pleasant Valley Road, Center City, Minn. 55012.

CHILDREN

Books and Other Recommended Materials

Imagination Press: Self-Help Books for Kids and the Adults in Their Lives, sponsored by the American Psychological Association, offers books on helping children understand their emotions, cope with separation from a parent, and other issues. Their Web site is www.maginationpress.com.

The following Web site can direct you to organizations and materials on parenting and helping children: www.helping.apa.org (American Psychological Association: Helping Children).

EMERGENCY MEDICAL SERVICE WORKERS

Unfortunately, to date, little has been written about emergency medical service workers. General readings on stress and on issues facing other men who work at at-risk jobs should be helpful.

FIREFIGHTERS

Resources

www.heroes-inc.org
National Fallen Firefighters Foundation: www.firehero.org

POLICE

Resources

International Union of Police Association: www.iupa.org

Books

Kates, A. 1999. *Copshock: Surviving Posttraumatic Stress Disorder (PTSD)*. Tucson, Ariz.: Holbrook Street Press.

MENTAL HEALTH TREATMENT

Books

Fanning, P., and M. McKay (Eds.). 2002. *Family Guide to Emotional Wellness*. Oakland, Calif.: New Harbinger Publications, Inc.

Organizations: Finding a Therapist or Treatment Program

In choosing a therapist or treatment program, you have the right to shop around and ask questions. Get recommendations from friends, doctors, and people who report having had positive therapeutic experiences; from hospitals with specialized treatment programs for the area of concern; the police; university health or counseling centers (if you are a student); and local mental health and social services agencies, which are usually run by either the city or county.

There are also local addiction and eating disorders treatment programs; local hotlines, local health centers, and local or state chapters of the Anxiety Disorders Association of America, the International Society for Traumatic Stress Studies, the American Psychiatric Association, the American Psychological Association, and the National Association of Social Workers. Any of these may also have lists of qualified professionals. If your partner is in the military, contact any of the military organizations listed below to inquire about mental health services.

Your telephone directory, local library, or social service agency can provide you with the phone numbers of the organizations listed here. If you contact any of these organizations, be sure to inquire if the therapist and programs are identified by speciality, such as depression.

THE MILITARY

Organizations Helping Active Duty Military Personnel and Their Families

Army

Army Family Team Building (AFTB):
www.armyfamilyteambulding.org
Army Community Service and Family Advocacy Programs:
www.goasc.org

Navy

Fleet and Family Support Division: www.lifelines.navy.mil

Marines

www.usmc.mil (then go to Family);
Marine Corps Community Service: www.usmc-mccs.org

Air Force

www.af.mil (then click on Questions and go to Tricare, or go directly to www.tricare.osd.mil; USAF Combat Support and Family Service

Organizations Helping Veterans and Their Families

Veterans and their families can seek assistance at their closest Department of Veterans Affairs Medical Center (VAMC) or Vet Center. Consult your local phone directory, library, or hospital to locate the nearest VAMC or Vet Center nearest you. Vet Centers may be listed in your telephone directory under "Vet Centers" or as "Veterans Outreach Centers."

Organizations such as the American Legion, Veterans of Foreign Wars, Paralyzed Veterans of America, Disabled American Veterans, and Blinded Veteran's Association help veterans and their families. Consult your local telephone directory or library, military service organization, or VAMC or Vet Center for a complete listing of these organizations and their locations.

Books

Mason, P. 1990. *Recovering from the War: A Woman's Guide to Helping Your Vietnam Vet, Your Family, and Yourself.* New York: Viking Press.

Matsakis, A. 1996. *Vietnam Wives: Facing the Challenges of Veterans Suffering from Post-Traumatic Stress,* 2nd ed. Baltimore, Md.: The Sidran Foundation.

Relationships

Books

Black, J., and G. Enns. 1998. *Better Boundaries: Owning and Treasuring Your Life.* Oakland, Calif.: New Harbinger Publications, Inc.

Gottman, J. M., and N. Silver. 1999. *The Seven Principles for Making Marriage Work.* New York: Three Rivers Press.

Hanson, P. 1991. *Survivors and Partners: Healing the Relationships of the Sexual Abuse Survivor.* Longmont, Colo.: Heron Hill Publishing Co.

Matsakis, A. 1996. *Trust After Trauma: A Guide to Relationships for Trauma Survivors and Those Who Love Them.* Oakland, Calif.: New Harbinger Publications, Inc.

SEX

Organizations

American Association of Sex Educators, Counselors, and Therapists (AASECT)

Few states issue a sex therapy license per se, so most people who specialize in this field are first licensed in something else, commonly psychology or social work. Then they seek certification from professional organizations to practice sex therapy. Distance sex therapy by phone or online is not recommended. There are no federal or state regulations on distance therapy of any type; no studies have been completed on its effectiveness; and there is no accountability either for clients or therapists.

Books

Westheimer, R. 1984. *Dr. Ruth's Guide to Good Sex.* New York: Warner Books.

Masters, W., and V. Johnson. 1970. *The Pleasure Bond: A New Look at Sexuality and Commitment.* Boston: Little Brown and Company.

RELAXATION, SELF-CALMING, AND SELF-CARE

Organizations

The Anxiety Disorders Association of America (ADAA), 1900 Parklawn Drive, Suite 100, Rockville, Md. 20852-2524. Web site: www.adaa.org.

Books

Bourne, E. 1995. *The Anxiety and Phobia Workbook*, 2nd ed. Oakland, Calif.: New Harbinger Publications, Inc.

_____. 2001. *Beyond Anxiety and Phobia.* Oakland, Calif.: New Harbinger Publications, Inc.

Davis, M., M. McKay, and E. Eshelman. 2000. *The Relaxation and Stress Reduction Workbook*, 5th ed. Oakland, Calif.: New Harbinger Publications, Inc.

McKay M., K. Beck, and C. Sutker. 2001. *The Self-Nourishment Companion: 52 Inspiring Ways to Take Care of Yourself.* Oakland, Calif.: New Harbinger Publications, Inc.

Gallo, F., and H. Vincenzi. 2000. *Energy Tapping: How to Rapidly Eliminate Anxiety, Depression, Cravings, and More Using Energy Psychology.* Oakland, Calif.: New Harbinger Publications, Inc.

TIME AND MONEY
Organizations

Help with credit card and debt reduction: The National Foundation for Credit Counseling (nonprofit) at www.nfcc.org or www.debtadvice.org, or 800-388-2227.

Help with mortgages, home equity, auto loans, problem credit, real estate issues, problem credit, CDs, savings, insurance, checking and financial management: www.bankrate.com

Books

Mayer, J. 1995. *Time Management for Dummies*, 1ˢᵗ ed. New York: Wiley Publishing.

Allen, D. 2001. *Getting Things Done: The Art of Stress-Free Production*. New York: Penguin Books.

Fanning, P., and H. G. Mitchener. 2001. *The 50 Best Ways to Simplify Your Life*. Oakland, Calif.: New Harbinger Publications, Inc.

Taylor-Houg, D. 2003. *Frugal Living for Dummies*. Hoboken, N.J.: Wiley Publishing.

Strauss, S., and A. Jaffei. *The Complete Idiot's Guide to Beating Debt*, 2ⁿᵈ ed. New York: Alpha Books.

TRAUMA-RECOVERY AND SYMPTOM MANAGEMENT
Recommended Books

Copeland, M. E. 2001. *The Depression Workbook: A Guide for Living with Depression and Manic Depression*, 2ⁿᵈ ed. Oakland, Calif.: New Harbinger Publications, Inc.

Matsakis, A. 1996. *I Can't Get Over It: A Handbook for Trauma Survivors*, 2ⁿᵈ ed. Oakland, Calif.: New Harbinger Publications, Inc.

Williams, M. B., and S. Poijula. 2002. *The PTSD Workbook: Simple, Effective Techniques for Overcoming Traumatic Stress Symptoms*. Oakland, Calif.: New Harbinger Publications, Inc.

References

Britt, D. 2003. Afraid that fear is here to stay. *The Washington Post*, Maryland and D.C. Edition. Metro B-1, B-4 (October 3).

Cameron, J. 1992. *The Artist's Way: A Spiritual Path to Higher Creativity*. New York: Jeremy P. Tarcher/Putnam.

Department of Defense. 2003a. U.S. Active Duty Military Deaths per 100,000 Serving—1980 through 2002, 2003. http://web1.whs. osd.mil/mmiodcasualtyucatas

Department of Defense. 2003b. Worldwide U.S. Active Duty Military Deaths: Deaths by Manner per 100,000 Strength. Figure 2. http://web1.whs.osd.mil/mmiodcasualtyucatas

The Economist. 1995. Comradeship. 336(7025):18-19 (July 29).

Gottman, J., and N. Silver. 1999. *The Seven Principles for Making Marriage Work*. New York: Three Rivers Press.

Hopkins, J., and C. Jones. 2003. Disturbing legacy of rescuers: Suicide. *USA Today*, pp. 13A, 14A (September 23).

Kates, A. 2001. *Copshock: Surviving Posttraumatic Stress Disorder (PTSD)*. Tucson, Ariz.: Holbrook Street Press.

Lamb, H., L. Weinberger, and L. DeCuir. 2002. The police and mental health. *Psychiatric Services* 53(10):1255-1271.

Langer, G. 2000. Use of antidepressants in a long-term practice. AMCNEWS.com. Retrieved from http://abcnews.go.com/onair/WorldNewsTonight/poll1000410.html April 10, 2000.

Laws, J. 2002. Fighting overconfidence. *Occupational Health and Safety* 71(8):4.

Maguire, B., K. Hunting, G, Smith, and N. Levick. 2002. Occupational fatalities in emergency medical services: A hidden crisis. *Annals of Emergency Medicine* 40(6):625-632.

Mason, P. 1990. *Recovering from the War: A Woman's Guide to Helping Your Vietnam Vet, Your Family, and Yourself*. New York: Viking Press.

Matsakis, A. 1996. *Vietnam Wives: Facing the Challenges of Veterans Suffering from Post-Traumatic Stress*, 2nd ed. Baltimore, Md.: The Sidran Foundation.

Maynard, P., N. Maynard, H. McCubbin, and D. Shao. 1980. Family life and the police profession: Coping patterns wives employ in managing job stress and the family environment. *Family Relations* 29:495-501.

Melzer, S. 2002. Gender, work and intimate violence: Men's occupational violence spillover and compensatory violence. *Journal of Marriage and the Family* 64(4):820-832.

Meyers, D. 2002. *Exploring Psychology*, 5th ed. New York: Worth Publishers.

Savoye, C. 2002. Fewer volunteers down at the local firehouse. *Christian Science Monitor* 92(56):2.

U.S. Census Bureau. 2002. *Statistical Abstract of the United States: Law Enforcement Officers Killed and Assaulted: 1990 to 2000*. Washington, D.C.

U.S. Fire Administration. 2003. Reports: Firefighter Fatality Retrospective Study 1990-2000. www.usfa.fema.gov/inside-usfa/nfdc/fa-220.shtm.

Van der Kolk, B., A. McFarlane, and L. Weiseath, Eds. 1996. *Traumatic Stress: The Effects of Overwhelming Stress on Mind, Body and Society.* New York: Guilford Press.

Winston, S. 2001. *What Every Trauma Therapist Should Know about Panic, Phobia, and OCD.* Audiotape 01ISTSS-71 ISTSS (International Society for Traumatic Stress Studies) 17th Annual Meeting, Fairmont Hotel, New Orleans, La., December, 2001.

Some Other
New Harbinger Titles

The Well-Ordered Office, Item 3856 $13.95

Talk to Me, Item 3317 $12.95

Romantic Intelligence, Item 3309 $15.95

Transformational Divorce, Item 3414 $13.95

The Rape Recovery Handbook, Item 3376 $15.95

Eating Mindfully, Item 3503 $13.95

Sex Talk, Item 2868 $12.95

Everyday Adventures for the Soul, Item 2981 $11.95

A Woman's Addiction Workbook, Item 2973 $18.95

The Daughter-In-Law's Survival Guide, Item 2817 $12.95

PMDD, Item 2833 $13.95

The Vulvodynia Survival Guide, Item 2914 $15.95

Love Tune-Ups, Item 2744 $10.95

The Deepest Blue, Item 2531 $13.95

The 50 Best Ways to Simplify Your Life, Item 2558 $11.95

Brave New You, Item 2590 $13.95

Loving Your Teenage Daughter, Item 2620 $14.95

The Hidden Feelings of Motherhood, Item 2485 $14.95

The Woman's Book of Sleep, Item 2418 $14.95

Pregnancy Stories, Item 2361 $14.95

The Women's Guide to Total Self-Esteem, Item 2418 $13.95

Thinking Pregnant, Item 2302 $13.95

The Conscious Bride, Item 2132 $12.95

Juicy Tomatoes, Item 2175 $13.95

Call **toll free, 1-800-748-6273,** or log on to our online bookstore at **www.newharbinger.com** to order. Have your Visa or Mastercard number ready. Or send a check for the titles you want to New Harbinger Publications, Inc., 5674 Shattuck Ave., Oakland, CA 94609. Include $4.50 for the first book and 75¢ for each additional book, to cover shipping and handling. (California residents please include appropriate sales tax.) Allow two to five weeks for delivery.

Prices subject to change without notice.